Children's Ministry

perspectives on

children and the gospel

perspectives on

children and the gospel

excellence in ministry with children and their families

Ron Buckland

Scripture Union

Scripture Union books are published in Australia by:
Scripture Union Resources for Ministry Unit
Unit 14 Cnr Gibbons & Nells Rd
West Gosford
NSW 2250
Australia

And in the United Kingdom by:
Scripture Union
207-209 Queensway
Bletchley, MK2 2 EB, England
www.scriptureunion.org.uk

The National Library of Australia Cataloguing-in-Publication entry

Buckland, Ron, 1938- .
Children and the Gospel : excellence in ministry with children and their families.

Bibliography.
ISBN 1 876794 13 5.

1. Christian education of children. 2. Children - Religious life.
I. Scripture Union Australia. II. Title.

268.432

Cover and text design by Kelvin Young, Preston, Victoria
Printed and bound in Australia by Openbook Publishers, Adelaide

contents

PART 1:

CONSIDERING CORE ISSUES

PART 2:

PUTTING IT ALL INTO PRACTICE

20 principles that lead to excellence.

preface

My friend, Ron Buckland, stands in a line of people who have been concerned with bringing the gospel to children. They have reckoned children to be different from adults, rather than smaller versions of them; hence their desire to bring the good news to children in a way that fits their situation.

The current debate brings three factors into focus: what the Scriptures say or infer about children; what the psychologists have observed and theorised about the development of children; and how the children's workers actually get across to children. There has been considerable enthusiasm and not a little heat in the exchanges since the late 60's.

Ron, the author of this book, has jumped into the whirlpool in all the above areas. In addition to numerous other youth ministries, he has interacted with children in lively and imaginative ways, talking with, writing for them, producing resources for them. And children have responded! He has kept abreast of relevant developmental studies and he has been alert in his attention to every new twist, over three decades, in the theology of childhood.

One of Ron's persistent emphases, which has undoubtedly irritated busy children's workers around the world, is that what you believe about the spiritual status of children must affect the way you present the gospel to them. Or put it the other way around: how you deal with children lays bare, for the discerning, your convictions about your theology of childhood. This needs to be said, clearly and persistently, and Ron has said it, both face-to-face, in conferences and consultations and in his two previous books.

Perhaps, however, we should also point to the following curious aspects of human inconsistency. There are some cases where a children's evangelist will proclaim, very strongly, that children are 'in the same boat' as adults, so far as repentance from an ungodly lifestyle, once-for-all definitive conversion and public confession of faith are concerned; and yet where the actual approach allows for developmental factors and responses in a way that belies the professed belief. A blessed blunder! But also there are those who agree mentally with all the emphases found in this book, but in the outcome, bring pressure to bear on the child's willingness to trust (where this applies) and extract confessions of faith on the slenderest biblical basis. Woe to this manipulative inconsistency!

Ron's style is clear, economic with words, and pungent as far as the current idioms of speech are concerned. Each chapter tackles a limited area, is sharply focused within that area and then finishes by attaching a 'hook', a link that makes transition easy to the next topic. The writing indeed has a deceptive simplicity about it. Constantly there are crisp sentences that reveal a sophisticated grasp of a contentious issue (whether theological, educational or in the realm of family studies) but also put a viewpoint that is fair, simple and defensible.

Another comment on style. Ron could scarcely be accused of writing poetic prose, but there is one thing in common between his prose and good poetry; the issue is displayed early, clearly and simply, and much meaning is poured into few words, and with no distraction in terms of footnotes or seductive by-paths. For these reasons it might even be described as intense, though 'focused' would probably fit better. It is as though he knows how little time we have to read, and so respects our limits.

I have noted that the book is far wider than theology in its scope, but would predict, nonetheless, that its impact on the theology of childhood will be considerable. It is an extraordinary thing that, in all the ramifications of theology over the last century, the question of childhood has featured so little. Perhaps denominational dogma has played a part here, closing off certain options as complicating in their effects. However this may be, it is as though the theological ostrich has buried its head in the 'too-hard basket'!

What Ron has done is to extract the central issues bluntly, if need be, from their ancient or contemporary surrounds, and to display them as an agenda for consideration. Not only so, but he has arrived at a defensible position on each, and formulated a 'big picture' or comprehensive theory overall. This is no mean achievement, and may well function as a 'point of departure' for later theologians, as John Pridmore's work did some years ago.

In the last thirty years Ron's theological views and mine on the question of childhood have had much in common, hammered out, as they were, in the context of Scripture Union, with its nineteenth century call to bring the gospel to children. And I now allow myself one digression: to salute Ron for the extraordinary contribution he has made to Scripture Union International, to the Pacific Region, to Scripture Union Tasmania; but particularly in his leadership of Scripture Union Australia over twenty eventful years. The thinker and writer was also the zestful doer.

At the moment Ron's views and mine do not converge completely, though we hold much in common. In particular, the points at issue seem to be the nature of the kingdom of God, the meaning of 'belonging' as applied to the persecuted, the poor and the children, and the doctrine of original sin. But we both continue to ask questions of each other, and hopefully learn more in the process.

I am happy, however, to affirm every one of Ron's '20 principles that lead to excellence' and would hope that every reader would ponder each one carefully. Each has been hammered out of experience and careful theological reflection, and taken together, they would give a sound basis for any practical course on children and the gospel.

In addition, despite the degree of divergence mentioned, Ron and I close ranks and stand shoulder to shoulder whenever we suspect that there is lack of respect for children, or worse, spiritual abuse or manipulation of children in the name of Christ and the gospel. Jesus' directive: 'Let the little children come to me', was given to his own undiscerning disciples but we suspect that, though in other times, in diverse circumstances and in different cultures, it disturbs and prompts us disciples to tell and to act in our world. We do so because of our love for him and for children.

Bill Andersen

PART 1

Considering Core Issues

Clearing the decks

This opening chapter has two purposes. First, to identify some of the issues around serious ministry with children. Second, to let you into some of the thinking of the author.

This book is, of course, biased. It has been written by a human being, all of whom are biased in some way or other. Some of the most dangerous people around are those who either believe they are not biased, or who know they are and won't tell you what the bias is. I am not sure which is the most dangerous. Both have caused havoc in Christian circles.

My bias includes at least the following factors:

(a) I am male.

(b) I am white.

(c) I am Anglo Saxon.

(d) I am 63.

(e) I am Australian.

(f) I am originally from Sydney.

(g) I now live in Melbourne.

(h) I have four degrees.

(i) I have been married for 33 years.

(j) I have two sons.

(k) I have been in 'full time' Christian ministry for over 30 years.

(l) I became a Christian at age 20.

(m) I have visited over 20 countries, and worked with people from a number of cultures.

Now there are some heavy influences in that lot! All of them have influenced who I am and what I am. The Holy Spirit continues to work on some of these influences, but a number keep impacting me. They influence in some way how I see the world, how I decide about reality, how priorities are set.

Then there are the personality factors, with which I will not bore you. My simple point is that I acknowledge bias, and that I am aware of some of it. So be patient with me, dear reader, and when/if you don't agree, allow for the fact of your own bias.

If these are some of the influences on me, let me share some of the passion that drives me, because a book about Christian ministry should not be dry and academic, even if it seeks to be intellectually worthwhile. One can be precise and passionate.

Do you want a reason, a strategy, for ministry with children? Do you need one?

The leaders of the world in the year 2030 are alive and well, and about 10 years old today.

The preachers, the politicians, the poets, the philosophers, the parents, the planners, are all there. So, potentially, are the pornographers, the perverts, the petty criminals, the pushers of drugs, and the polluters. (There are even some for both lists that don't start with 'p'!).

What we do now in ministry with children has the potential to change our world. God, by his Spirit, will bring about any change that lasts. That is acknowledged and true. But for his own reasons, God has chosen to allow us to be partners in the gospel, co-workers, giving to us a ministry of reconciliation (2 Corinthians 5:18).

The children you parent, meet, teach and influence, will lead the world - little bits of it, or big bits of it, later. Let us be committed to the idea that nothing we do now will have to be apologised for and undone later. To put that more positively, that we so carry out our bit of ministry with children now that others will be able to build straight onto it, and that the children themselves will be empowered by our ministry to know how to go forward with God.

Because be assured at the outset, this is a book about evangelism amongst children. That does not mean there will be nothing about the nurture of children in Christian understanding and behaviour. The relationship between evangelism and nurture will become clearer as we go along.

There is a relationship - they are not opposed, and must not be separated from each other. One of the least helpful lines of thought I encountered in theological training days was the idea that in the Acts of the Apostles we see that the early church first evangelised, then taught. There were Greek words associated with both ideas, of course, but the basic idea is clear.

The fact is that for the early Christians their evangelism was in their teaching, and their teaching was evangelistic. It stands to reason, if we stop and think about it for a minute. You don't have to know much to be a Christian, but you have to know something. There has to be some basis for faith. Becoming a Christian is not about how much you know, but about what you do with the knowledge you have, in relation to Jesus Christ.

Any human being who receives information does something with it. They might suppress it; they might twist it and make it fit into their present framework of thinking. They might even realise that there needs to be a change of some kind if they are to accommodate the reality they have just acknowledged. But they will do something with it. Every human being does this, at every age.

So, when people ask, 'Can a child respond to the gospel?', they are asking what is really a 'non - question'. The child will respond to any information received. The question is not 'Can a child respond?', but 'What response is the child giving?' Now, that is a very different question, and it means that anyone reading this is involved in the great challenge, and the wonderful privilege, of carefully 'tuning in' to the responses being given by any child with whom they minister.

What can children understand?

As we set out on this journey, there are at least two things about ministry with children that need to be said straight away. The first is that if we get serious about such a ministry, we will have some hard thinking to do, because any ministry with children that wants to be excellent will have to deal with tough questions about children and God, conversion, sin, repentance and faith. That list is not exhaustive. As we will find out, if we start to think about children's ministry seriously, we touch almost every aspect of Christian thinking.

Secondly we will see that if anyone writing about this ministry is to say something fresh and practical, they will have to be willing to 'stick their neck out' sometimes. Positions will need to be taken, if we are to avoid bland descriptions of alternative positions. Sometimes we need to know there are other ways of seeing things, and sometimes different approaches can be equally valid. But often we need to be willing to stand apart and say that 'the emperor has no clothes'.

Do you know the story from which that saying came? It is very funny. Some men wanted to trick a vain despot. They convinced him that the 'invisible' clothing they could supply was superior to anything else. The stupid man paraded naked through his city, and his courtiers were so afraid they went along with it, praising the superior clothing and the vain king. Until a child called out, 'but he has no clothes on!' (It was a child, of course!)

Sometimes it is necessary to speak strongly about conclusions taken for granted because no one has looked at their foundations for a while. I am about to do that on the matter of children and their capacity to understand.

Almost all training events for adults involved in ministry with children will include an elective on 'the ages and stages of children'. I have conducted a number myself. In many I have heard the trainer outline theories of child development, according to some 'great one', and then make practical applications about what children of different ages 'can and cannot do'. It all seems so logical and neat. Which is its problem, of course.

Let me be clear at the outset. The insights of childhood studies can help us to understand some of the broad aspects of the normal development of children. But they never describe a real child. Trainers can be dealing with 'abstract' children in their courses, not the real, red-blooded kids we actually encounter. So I see insights from child development studies as of limited, but strategic, help. I see the 'enthronement' of such ideas as ruinous to the ideas themselves and unhelpful to ministry with real children.

That there are limitations in the capacity of children, especially little children, is beyond question. What we adults have so often failed to ask is whose limitations are being disclosed. Let me explain.

If asked in a setting of trust, many children will draw a picture of their understanding of what God looks like. What they usually produce is a variation of the dignified old man on a throne in the sky. One American researcher, Victor Pitts, can tell the denomination of the child from the drawing of God produced! Which sounds odd, until one thinks about it a bit. It is highly likely that a child will reproduce 'God' according to the main descriptions heard in their church circles. In fact, the 'old man' images come out of the attempts of adults to 'explain' God in ways a child can grasp. When we call God 'he' and a 'Father', we have pushed a child strongly in the direction of the 'old man'.

God is, of course, the 'Eternal Father' (Isaiah 9:6). He is, eternally, the Father of our Lord, Jesus Christ. But the Bible never teaches that God is like our human father. Yet people regularly will say this to children: 'God is like a father to you'. Imagine the impact on a child who only knew a drunken, violent, molesting father.

What the Bible teaches is that our human father should be like God, which is a very different line of thought! To round off this point, it needs to said that the Bible never argues from earth to heaven, always the other way around. So, in Ephesians 5 Paul does not say that the relationship between Christ and the church is like that of a husband with a wife. He says the opposite: that the husband/wife relationship should be like that of Christ with his church. We need to be very careful with the use of biblical pictures and metaphors, separating out what is reality and what is picture, then applying it all in the right direction!

For example, God is a Father, of our Lord Jesus Christ. That is a reality. We can call him 'Father' as a result of adoption, based on our status 'in Christ.' That is reality. But Jesus did not teach a general 'fatherhood' of God. In fact, he consistently distinguished between 'my Father' and his disciples' link to God (for example in John 14:1-14). Some will point out that the 'Lord's Prayer' starts with 'Our Father'. But Jesus was responding to the request, 'Teach us how to pray'. He said to the disciples, 'When you pray, say "Our Father"'. It was only after the resurrection that he spoke about 'my Father and your Father', as he drove home to our minds the new reality he had brought into the world (John 20:17).

We have taken time with this, because the idea that God is like our father still gets airplay. The metaphors we use with children need to be carefully tested, especially when we claim they come from the Bible. There are powerful pictures in Scripture, as the writers struggled to convey reality that often defied language.

Our use of them will need to stay true to what is said, and to take account of the capacity of a child. So, if we get serious about excellent children's ministry, we will face the challenge of hermeneutics (the science of interpreting the Bible).

Let's return to the drawing of 'God'. This is an example of 'concrete ' thinking, which can be defined as that thinking for which a picture can be drawn. 'Abstract' thinking can't be drawn. 'Faith', as an idea, is abstract. It can be described in action, but the reality of 'faith' is something different from the description of it in action. It is the same with 'love' and 'courage', and lots of other great ideas.

Most people will display both kinds of thinking throughout their lives. Some say quite dogmatically that children are not capable of abstract thought. This view suggests that children cannot understand what they say they believe. The position is often reinforced by 'funny kids' moments' in church circles. As we look at a couple of these, take note how often what children say is based on a mishearing or a misunderstanding of what adults have said.

'This morning we will preach the gossip.'

'What comes after Judges?' 'Policemen!'

As the plane gained altitude four-year-old Steve said, 'I hope we don't bump into Jesus.'

A five-year-old shooting his popgun at the sky explained he was trying to shoot God down 'because I don't want him watching me all the time.'

Perhaps these childish interpretations are not as funny as we think. Children use the same process to think about spiritual realities as they do to grapple with any other part of their world. Look at this example:

Five-year-old Lynn was asked,

'If God is not a man (which she interpreted as to be an adult) what else could he be?' After careful thought she concluded,

'He must be a little child.'

Since thinking of God as an animal was repugnant to Lynn, she concluded that God must be another-sized human being.

That is not a bad piece of reasoning, especially in response to a clumsily put adult question. In an important book published in 1978, Margaret Donaldson made much about the manner in which adults ask questions of children. Her concern, as an educationalist, was to find out why the lively pre-school child so often becomes a semi-literate and defeated 'school failure'. Her research showed how often we underestimate the thinking powers of the young child.

Donaldson is significant because she quietly but firmly overturned many of the assumptions about children and thinking based on the work of Jean Piaget. This Swiss psychologist put forward the idea that children pass through four major 'stages' in the development of their capacity to think. He identified the four stages, and the approximate ages associated with them, based on experiments in which children solved puzzling situations.

What Donaldson did was to redo all the main puzzle situations, asking more carefully worded questions to the children. The children she worked with consistently showed levels of thinking of which they were not capable, according to Piaget. Which showed that his conclusions had been mainly about the inability of adults to so enter the world of a child that they could ask questions in ways that children actually do understand what the task is!

This is not to say that Piaget was totally wrong, and that there are no 'stage-like' steps in the development of the thinking of a human being. Little children do mainly think concretely. But to say that they cannot think abstractly is to go too far. They can, but they can't stay there. The typical adult can think abstractly. But not many can stay there all the time. They need a dose of concrete thinking from time to time! How many churchgoers remember the story that illustrated the sermon's main theme, and not the theme! Or the children's talk!

The call of this book is not to underestimate children and their capacities. We have done that for too long in Christian circles. We have too often been childish in our dealings with our children. To explain the meaning of the death of Christ to an eight-year-old is a challenge worth accepting. To deal with it using only metaphors and object lessons, instead of straight biblical teaching, is to belittle the child. One suspects it has often been the 'soft option' for adults in a hurry.

The way to check what a child is understanding is to ask them! Or to let them ask us! That is, teaching children must become genuine dialogue if it is to be teaching of excellence. Questions are a teacher's best friend, something you would not believe watching too many teachers handle children who want to ask questions. Over and over I have seen adults fail to deal with the questions of children. Sometimes it is because the adults don't spend the time needed to understand what question is being asked. It is the essence of love to carefully tune in to what is actually on another person's mind before offering an 'answer' to them.

Sometimes adults don't answer children's questions because they are too busy reaching their own goals. A simple question to ask ourselves in any teaching ministry with children is: Are we there to teach the children or the curriculum? Some would say that it is not an either/or choice: that we teach the curriculum to the children. But what if your group of children really does show enthusiasm for knowledge off to the side of the curriculum themes? What if a child asks a question in a session, one that is to one side of the theme, but is clearly of huge interest to all the children?

An excellent teacher will 'go with the flow'. This is not an anti-curriculum comment. Curriculums are fine, but they have to be general. No one can produce material for every situation: the designers of curriculum expect you to adapt what they have supplied, to fit your kids. I am saying that if your group, from time to time, goes 'sideways' by their questions, go with them. Any worthwhile curriculum will be in units anyway, so the theme of the unit will be taken up again next week.

This is a chapter about children and their understanding, not just their thinking. Understanding includes imagination. Imagination includes thinking, but is more. In RE classes I sometimes talk with the children about 'thinking, and thinking about thinking'. I tell them that when we think about what we are thinking about, we are beginning to use our imaginations. I find this not a bad starting point, and the children seem to agree!

We are going to have to use our imagination if we are to grasp anything true about God. He is a reality beyond our thinking, but not beyond our imagining, if that imagining is shaped by truth. It is through Scripture that God informs the Christian mind, enabling us to imagine God truthfully. 'The Scriptures are not something we look at, but rather something we look through.' John Calvin, a very famous leader of the 16th Century Protestant Reformation, once wrote:

'Just as old or bleary-eyed men and those with weak vision, if you thrust before them a most beautiful volume, even if they recognize it to be some form of writing, yet can scarcely construe two words, but with aid of spectacles will begin to read distinctly, so Scripture, gathering up the otherwise confused knowledge of our minds, having dispersed our dullness, clearly shows us the true God.'

I think the spectacles God uses are the work of the Holy Spirit on our imaginations. So, when 2 Corinthians 4: 6 says God 'has shone in our hearts to give the light of the knowledge of the glory of God in the face of Christ', 'heart' is one way of speaking about our imagination.

Calvin was writing about adults. The pity is that so many adults see imagination as a childish thing. They will acknowledge, for example, that C S Lewis's Narnia series is a work of great imagination, but see it only as children's literature. Adults, the 'doorkeepers' to the lives of children in so many ways, will continue to trivialize imagination in their own minds as long as they see it only, or mainly, as a 'childish' faculty. Adults will miss the central role imagination could/should have in their own faith development.

With all of this in mind, I want to finish this chapter by placing alongside each other two examples of the use of imagination in writing for children. There is a bad use of imagination, as well as good uses of this God-given faculty. Some uses of imagination hold children back in their journey with God. It is not simply the use of imagination that is the issue, but use of the kind of imagination that helps children move forward, not backwards, in their spirituality.

Here is the opening of a book, part of a series which aims to provide 'Christian reading' for primary aged children, especially girls.

"'Don't get too close, Amanda. You might fall in.'

Her mother grasped the back of her long, dark skirt. Mandie tried to pull free. Her tear-filled blue eyes sought a glimpse of her father through the homemade wooden coffin resting by the open grave.

'I want to go with you, Daddy!' she was mumbling to herself.

'Take me with you, Daddy!'

She tugged at her long, blond braid in her grief. Even in her sadness she was afraid of being scolded by her stern mother. She dared not cry out in anguish. Her voice trembled as she whispered,

'How can I live without you, Daddy? You were the only one who ever loved me. I can't bear it alone!'

Preacher DeHart's deep voice echoed throughout the hills.

'We all know Jim Shaw was a good man. He drew his last breath talking to God. We trust his soul is at peace.'

His voice grew louder and more emphatic.

'But, friends and loved ones, I am here to remind you of one thing! When the time comes for you to face your Maker, you will be damned to hellfire and brimstone if you have lived a sinful life!'

Mandie trembled as she heard the words.

'You will incur the wrath of God and your soul will burn in hell for evermore,' he continued.

'Above all, let us remember the Ten Commandments and keep them holy, live by them and walk the narrow path in preparation for the hereafter. Otherwise, I admonish you, your soul will burn in hell! Your soul will be used to feed the fires of the Devil! When you have sinned and come short of the glory of God, he will forsake you. He will punish you!'

The child was overcome by fear and grief as the final words were said for her father and the coffin was lowered into the ground. The clods of mountain earth hit the casket with a thud. She gasped for breath and, falling on her knees beside the grave, she appealed to God,

'What have I done to cause you to take my daddy away, God? I love him so much, dear God!'"

Apart from the appalling level of writing (and the amazing overuse of exclamation marks!), this is a terrible example, still in print, of what happens when the imagination is manipulated instead of 'massaged'.

In total contrast are the Narnia series by C S Lewis. Here the arrival of Aslan is anticipated with an imagination that 'flies':

"'You'll be interested when you see him.'

'But shall we see him?' asked Susan.

'Why, daughter of Eve, that's what I brought you here for. I'm to lead you to where you shall meet him,' said Mr Beaver.

'Is - is he a man?' asked Lucy.

'Aslan a man!' said Mr Beaver sternly. 'Certainly not. I tell you he is the King of the wood and son of the great Emperor-beyond the-sea. Don't you know who is King of the Beasts? Aslan is a lion -the Lion, the great Lion.'

'Ooh!' said Lucy, 'I'd thought he was a man. Is he - quite safe? I shall feel rather nervous about meeting a lion.'

'Safe?' said Mrs Beaver. 'Who said anything about safe?' 'Course he isn't safe. But he's good. He's the King, I tell you.'"

Which piece of writing would you want to use with your children?!

Childhood: an endangered species?

'The society that neglects its children is one generation away from destruction.'

This penetrating statement was made by a famous researcher, Margaret Mead. It remains true as an insight, one that should sober us adults, because our societies continue to be inconsistent in our attitudes and behaviour towards childhood. We can bring tears to the eyes of any audience of adults by talking softly and warmly about children. I saw it again last night on TV. And many politicians will tell us that 'our children are our greatest asset', even outside an election year!

We do think our kids matter, as a society. But, at the same time, we let them be exploited, abused and manipulated as if they did not matter. Why did it take so long to get extradition agreements with other countries about paedophiles? Why do we allow younger and younger children to become models on TV? Why do we allow child slavery to continue at all, anywhere in the world?

What follows are some statistics, and some quotes from various sources, illustrative of the idea that childhood, so quickly put on a pedestal, is actually in some danger.

*The Anti-Slavery Society estimates that there are 100 million child-labourers worldwide; the United Nations puts the total at 145 million.

*It is estimated that there are something between 175 and 200 million child prostitutes throughout the world.

*In Washington (USA) 11-year-olds wear beepers to school to

receive drug assignments. They are used as go-betweens because it is hard to put them in gaol. The children make several hundred dollars a day.

*'Torture a kid and you stop him feeling anyone's pain but his own. Eventually, he'll hit back, at someone else, and when he's locked up, it's like a breeder reactor - prison turns him into nuclear waste, and it's too late.'

*'I've seen 5-year-old, sexually trained human beings. That tiny child who already knows that the way to avoid pain is to provide sex has almost no chance of growing up and being a proper human being.'

*'A lot of these men have children of their own and I wonder what they do to their own children if they are willing to do these things to other people's.'

*12-year-old Patricio Hilario da Silva's body was found on a main street in Ipanema, Brazil, with a hand - written note around his neck: 'I killed you because you didn't study and had no future. The government must not allow the streets of this city to be invaded by kids like you.'

*Melissa is a runaway who had been abused sexually at home over a long period. Once, working as a child prostitute, she got in a car and dealt with the man's sexual wants, then he dropped her off hastily. He had to hurry, he told Melissa, because his daughter had a part in the eighth-grade play and she would be terribly unhappy if her daddy was late.

*A monitored phone call by Los Angeles police:

'I want a girl of ten years.'

'A little girl of ten years?'

'Yes. Perfect. Also one of eight years and six years....'

'I think I can find a girl of ten, but if I can find someone younger I'll try.'

'OK.'

'OK. And you want to have sex with her?'

'Yes, yes. And I want to have, if possible, hard sex.'

'Very hard sex?'

'OK. We can do all this?'

'You can do anything you want with her.'

'After she make love, she die.'

'Do you want to kill the girl?'

'Yes. What happens when she die?'

'We would have to find a way to get rid of the body.'

'Aha. And how much would that cost?'

(In this case, it cost the paedophile life imprisonment.)

Did you know that childhood, as a separate life experience, is a reasonably recent 'invention'? In ancient societies people were regarded as infants until they were about seven years old. Then there was an initiation ceremony of some kind (usually painful), after which they entered the adult world of (hard) work.

If you look at paintings from, say, the Middle Ages, you will see children shown as little adults. They are dressed the same way as adults. They took part in festivals alongside adults. They were held to be responsible before the law. (A seven-year-old could be hanged for stealing in Tudor England.)

Homes in the Middle Ages were not divided into special rooms, for example, for sleeping, or eating. So children could not escape the adult world, of which they were part anyway. And adults, including parents, showed an attitude towards children that we find shocking, until we remember that so many children died in those days. Up to the Seventeenth Century, 75% (!) of all children christened were dead before the age of five. In that kind of setting, to survive emotionally one had to keep children 'at a distance'. One developed a degree of emotional detachment. 'I have lost three children in their infancy not without regret, but without great sorrow', wrote one famous 17th Century European.

Rapid changes took place in childhood after the 17th Century. There were several reasons for this. One was religious. Children in the Middle Ages knew the 'facts of life' before they could walk, understandable in houses in which everything happened in one big room. People began to believe that children start out in life 'innocent' and should be kept that way as long as possible. 'Innocence' was a religious understanding.

Another force for change was economics. In feudal society the lord and serf could be illiterate together, but as trade and commerce grew literacy of some sort was demanded. You had to be able to count and to read some things, or you would be cheated. So education became more systematic. For example, children began to be divided up into classes of the same age group. Other reforms reinforced the idea of separate worlds, often trying to preserve 'innocence' as long as possible. Harrow, the famous English school, banned drinking, fornication and gambling - the mind boggles at what the situation was like before the bans!

By the end of the 19th Century upper class children were even segregated in the home, forbidden to most of the house and only seeing their parents at certain times. They also now had special kinds of clothes, the sort of flouncing, fluffy clothes that were completely unlike adult clothes. Lower class children still, however, lived in the adult world. In Victorian London or Paris they drank, gambled, were active sexually and worked long hard hours. So with lower class children, the bond between parents and children was still largely economic, while in the upper classes the bond between children and parents had become emotional. As time passed the attitudes operating in the upper classes seeped into the other classes as well.

It is Victorian ideas that have affected most of the 20th Century in Western countries, and countries strongly influenced by the West (which is most countries, including those opposed to the idea!). But there was a strange dimension to the Victorian attitude towards children. Here is a quotation from Philip Greven, *The Protestant Temperament* that captures the paradox:

'When children are regarded mainly as miniature adults, no one can expect them to be cherished with particular care. But when they are studied and petted and admired, in some cases wept over and exalted as saints, the partial survival of brutality and disdain towards children is surprising. And this is the curious paradox, the chief distinguishing characteristic, of Victorian parent -child relations: that within one society - sometimes within one particular person, tenderness and even cloying affection could coexist with fierce discipline and a brooding suspicion of sin. Harshness to children had always existed; but seldom, as in the Victorian period, combined with curiosity and love.'

Why spend time on attitudes in Victorian England in a book on children at the start of the 21st Century? Because the whole of the 20th Century has seen these two, paradoxical, attitudes present. They have created confusion about childhood and its place in society. We still haven't worked it out. Meanwhile, at every level: home, school, courts, parliaments and church, we disclose our confusion in attitude and in actions.

For example, when the UN passed a Charter on the Rights of the Child, Australia signed it. In doing so we apparently agreed that children were people who needed to be accorded fundamental rights, alongside appropriate responsibilities. But because some people feared the loss of parental control over children, and alleged that the Charter attacked that control, Australia had still not acted on its ratification nearly 20 years later!

This example illustrates the two themes of Victorian attitudes towards children. One stream emphasises the child's capacity for good, and so encourages anything that empowers the child for personal action. The other stream emphasises the child's capacity for evil, and so encourages anything that will help work against this, including control of the child's decision making.

These streams can be linked to two legacies, two names, which provided the focus for each one: Jean-Jacques Rousseau and John Wesley. Both were men of the 18th Century whose ideas and influence shaped thinking about children in the 19th Century. That thinking flowed over into the 20th Century and now on into the 21st.

First, let us consider the influence of Wesley. When the 'Wesleyan Revival' came to England in the 18th Century, it represented a return to the past in its attitude to children. It was specifically, a return to a Puritan past. The 17th Century Puritans had seen a child's disobedience as an affront to God, and as an outworking of the fact that the child had been 'conceived in sin'. Because childhood was the opposite of being virtuous, it was a phase to be moved through as quickly as possible. The longer the period before conversion, the greater the danger of being damned. Infant death was still high, so childhood was a dangerous time, spiritually as well as physically. There was a belief in childhood conversion, the major sign of which was the turning away from all frivolity. Literature for children of the period portrayed these 'infant saints'.

John Wesley was convinced of the need to 'break the will of the child'. The innate 'depravity' (meaning that all parts of the child's life were affected by sin) made the matter urgent. So, one of the streams of thought about children which came into this century via John Wesley was based on the idea that children are incapable of good. This is because of the child's incorporation into the sin of Adam. The shorthand for what is in mind was 'original sin'. We will look at this idea in the next chapter.

Rousseau's position was based on the opposite idea. He believed that children were incapable of evil, until they were influenced by adults. This 'cult of childhood innocence' was also linked to a particular interpretation of biblical teaching, like Matthew 18:3:

'unless you change and become like little children you will never enter the kingdom of heaven'.

But, as one writer has said, 'One could almost write the history of attitudes to childhood by charting the changing ways people have interpreted a text like Matthew 18:3'.

Not only did Rousseau hold that children are naturally pure, he also said that they are utterly different (different in kind) from adults. So he questioned everything that was built on the idea that children are really little adults. He was directly opposed to the idea that wilfulness in children had to be addressed. The idea that a child's will would have to be broken was repugnant to those who follow his thinking.

Here, then, are two major influences about childhood that have flowed into our time and into our thinking. There is a 'Puritan' influence, which believed devoutly in original sin and in the need to break the will of the child. This influence would give more power to parents, would warn against moral laxness, and would strive to make children fit into the world of responsible adults.

On the other hand, there is the 'Romantic' influence, which believed in the natural goodness of children, and suggested they might be wiser than adults. This influence would give more freedom to children, would protest against severity and would argue that the ways and ideas of the young were as good, maybe better, than the rigid approach of adults.

The interesting thing is that both influences are present today, at the same time, about the same children. We want to put them on a pedestal, and keep them in their place, both at the same time. In fact, one of the great challenges today is the loss of childhood for so many children. This historical excursion has helped us see that the idea that there is a 'childhood' to lose is, itself, a relatively recent thing. The upsetting quotes at the start of this chapter reminded us that too many children have actually lost their childhood.

We do not have to be controlled by past influences, but we will be if we do not know what they are. Even to have the ambition to 'be biblical', which I have, is not, of itself, enough to protect us from control by the past. I don't want to follow either Wesley or Rousseau, but I will (or some variation of them) if I don't understand their influence on me and my times.

It may be easier to find children innocent and refreshing in times of relative prosperity, when we are more confident that our work is making the future brighter. Maybe in times of decline we are more likely to find children a liability.

'The arrival of children constitutes the gravest crisis that the average marriage encounters'.

There is an upsurge in pet ownership in times of economic downturns!

Even if economics is not the major factor, the fact remains that we have a contradictory attitude towards children in our society. In the ads that feature them (maybe itself part of the problem?) a positive image comes across. But our attitude towards the real children we know is often fairly negative. We know that they are not 'little angels', and they need to 'know their place', not getting too big-headed. In some twisted way, many adults seem to seek, and need, the approval of children - even their own children. No wonder the kids are confused!

One of life's joys is to look into the bright eyes of a child full of hope and life. One of the most stomach-turning experiences we can have is to look into young eyes that are dead of hope, hurting, suspicious, hating, calculating.

As I write this, I have just received a mailing from World Vision. In it is the announcement of establishment of 'The Global Movement For Children'. This Movement is a 'collective global force of organisations and individuals who are dedicated to working together to stimulate worldwide commitment to children's rights.' There was to be a special session of the United Nations in September 2001, to review progress made towards the goals set at the World Summit for Children in 1989. This session has been postponed because of the September 11, 2001 terrorist attacks. It should be a reasonably sober session: whilst some progress has been made, there is a long way to go. Why not contact your local World Vision office and connect with the Global Movement for Children?

We live with the reality of humanity's rebellion against God. Sin, and its tragic outworking, catches us all up in some way or another. That is agreed. But what do we say about children, even quite young children, whose experience of life is so terrible and so traumatic that they have never really been allowed to be children? Some would argue that such children are more 'sinned against' than sinners. It all depends what you believe about sin, so to that subject we turn.

Children and sin

For those who look to the Bible as their authority for matters to do with God, Romans chapter 5 is very important when we think about sin, especially as it relates to children. Verse 12 is a key, which reads in the New International Version:

'Therefore, just as sin entered the world through one man, and death through sin, and in this way death passed to all men, because all sinned.'

The 'one man' through whom sin entered the world is Adam. Paul will go on in the chapter to compare and contrast Adam with another 'one man' (Jesus Christ), through whom something greater than sin (the gift that came from grace; being made right with God; eternal life) entered the world. So keep in mind that Paul's main concern is Jesus, not Adam. And that he is contrasting them, not equating them. However, he does say some things about Adam:

(a) sin, which already existed, got into the human world through Adam's action.

(b) death rode into our world through sin.

Now comes the tricky bit. We need to know that what we are about to tackle has produced a little mountain of writing, lots of controversy and had people branded as heretics from time to time in the church's history. So we need to tread carefully, but we need to tread. The mishandling of this passage has caused a lot of unnecessary heartache to parents, pastors and individual people.

Paul either goes on to say:

* sin and death passes to all people as they line up with Adam's sin. or:

* sin and death passed to all people when Adam sinned.

Let's deal with the second idea first, that is, that I am caught up in sin and its consequences (death) because of Adam. In some way he has become 'head' of the human race. At the moment Adam sinned, every person sinned. It is not a question of me choosing to sin - I am sinful, and will therefore choose to sin. To put that another way, I may see myself choosing to sin, but the fact is that I have a bias towards sin because of my link to Adam. As a result, I cannot choose not to sin, at any age. I am a human being outside of Christ.

A famous Christian thinker, very influential in the Western church, was Augustine, bishop of Hippo (a place in North Africa). Augustine lived in the fourth century of the Christian era, when sin had become a bit of an issue. A lot of the agenda had to do with baptism, especially the baptism of babies or infants. People were baptising infants all over the place, and some began to ask why. Were babies being baptised because otherwise they were 'lost'? That seemed the most logical explanation, given that it was generally agreed that baptism was for the washing away of sin, to allow entry into the kingdom of God as a cleansed and forgiven person.

Augustine strongly believed this. An earlier writer (Cyprian) had talked about 'original sin', and Augustine picked this up. He did so in the midst of conflict. A man called Pelagius denied that the original sin of Adam was transmitted automatically to everyone, as babies. Augustine wrote against this teaching. He argued that Jesus could not be the Saviour of infants if they have nothing from which to be saved. He was sure they did, because he believed that all human beings sinned 'in Adam'. And if we all sinned 'in Adam', we are condemned with Adam. That condemnation comes with human life. At conception we begin human life and at the same time enter into sin and its consequences.

We need to know that Augustine based a lot of this on a particular translation of Romans 5:12. It read:

'Therefore as through one man sin entered into the world and through sin death, so also death passed to all men, because in him all sinned.'

Do you see the key phrase? 'In him', that is, 'in Adam' we all sinned. Now we need to know that this phrase is not in the original Greek text of Romans. Augustine apparently did not read Greek. He worked from Latin. The important little Greek phrase 'ef ho' (because, inasmuch) became 'en quo' (in whom) in the Latin version of the text. One writer says that 'Augustine's whole doctrine of original sin and inherited guilt was founded on this mistranslation'. Once we have humanity locked into a 'federal head' whose actions have outcomes that control all of us, the question of sin and the child is settled. Every child is caught up in Adam's sin, and is sinful, in need of salvation. Those who want to follow up how Christian leaders, including Augustine, have thought about children over the years, will find this publication useful: *The Child in Christian Thought*, edited by Marcia J Bunge, Eerdmans 2001.

This is not just dry academic stuff. If I am a parent with a little child who is likely to die, I passionately want to know about the eternal destiny of my child. In the fourth century, life was short for many people, and the death rate amongst babies was appalling. If your answer is that my baby will go to hell because of Adam's sin, I am stricken and want to know what can be done about it. If you tell me that the baptism of my baby will provide an answer, I will do it.

So did infant baptism arise because of an increasing understanding of 'original sin', or did 'original sin' come from infant baptism? One writer says bluntly:

'There is no doubt that the custom of infant baptism was the single most powerful catalyst of the formulation of doctrines of original sin ... The church baptises babies who, it is agreed, have not sinned in their own person; therefore, we must believe that they are baptised for the cleansing or remission of original sin. Original sin must be part of the faith of the church; why else does the church baptise babies?'

Let me remind you where we are. In Romans 5:12 Paul says a number of things about sin, death and the world. He says that sin came into the world through the action of Adam. He says death came into the world through that sin. He says that all people are caught up in this because...

either: sin and death passed to us all when Adam sinned.

or: sin and death pass to us when we line up with Adam's sin.

Let's now look at this second idea. If the first idea means automatic sinfulness, does this second idea mean that we may never sin? We have been affected by the rebellion of Adam. Christian orthodoxy has taught that we have a bias towards sin. But if sin is something one chooses to do, there must be awareness in the chooser. It may be more likely than less likely that we will sin, but we are not puppets or computers, programmed for destruction. God has built into us the capacity to choose. The exercise of that capacity is awesome. It affects our eternal destiny, and we are accountable for what we do with it. If we choose to line up with the sinful rebellion of Adam, we will face the consequences of that choice.

This emphasis on choice is not accidental, of course. One of the ways a little child is defined in the Bible has to do with the capacity to choose.

In Deuteronomy 1:39, Moses is passing on some things that God has said about the Promised Land. God says to the people that 'the little ones ... your children who do not yet know good from bad' will enter the land. This is said in the context of telling the people who chose against God that they will not enter the land. In passing, it seems that the only basis for the entry of the 'little ones' is that they are 'little ones'. They are not getting in because they obeyed - the whole point is to contrast them with those who chose not to obey. Maybe God is saying that the kingdom belongs to little ones like these, just because they are little ones. Jesus taught the same thing, as we will see in a later chapter.

In Isaiah 7:15-16 the prophet is speaking a warning message from God. He wants to make the point that what he is talking about will happen soon. So he says that before the child he is describing 'knows enough to reject the wrong and choose the right' it will happen. If we put these two Old Testament passages together, we get a glimpse of an understanding about the status of a child before God that is based on the ability to choose. There seems to be a time before which the child will not be held accountable, and a time after which they will be accountable. The difference seems less like a moment than a capacity which would grow over time, a capacity to tell the difference between good and evil, alongside an ability and will to choose one or the other.

Now let's go back to Romans 5:12. The fact that Adam's actions affect all humanity seems plain. We are born into a world characterised by sin and rebellion against God. We are also born with a 'twist' in our human nature, one that left alone will result in our own rebellion against God. But the 'twist' or bias is not automatic. We choose to obey or disobey God. When we choose to disobey God, we line up with Adam's sin. Even if we believe that all human beings will do that, that is, they will choose sin and therefore need salvation, the status of a child before the conscious choice can be made is left open. It is left open to the grace of God, which is not the worst thing in the world to be left with!

So let us do some thinking about the status of the child before God.

Jesus about children

We will start our discussion of the status of the child by looking at what Jesus said about children.

There is little reported contact between Jesus and children in the gospels: not none, but not a lot. He may have had a lot more to do with children than the gospel writers recorded. They could not record everything, as John reminds us (John 20:30). Each writer had his own portrait of Jesus to paint, with limited space to use.

But one encounter between Jesus and children is recorded in each of the three so-called 'Synoptic' gospels. (The gospels of Matthew, Mark and Luke are called 'synoptic' because they can be placed alongside each other. They are not the same, but there are many similarities.)

This is the incident when children are brought to Jesus and he compared them to those adults who seek the kingdom of God.

Mark's version of this meeting is in chapter 10, verses 13 to 16:

'People were bringing little children to Jesus to have him touch them, but the disciples rebuked them. When Jesus saw this, he was indignant. He said to them, "Let the little children come to me, and do not hinder them, for the kingdom of God belongs to such as these. I tell you the truth, anyone who will not receive the kingdom of God like a little child will never enter it." And he took the children in his arms, put his hands on them and blessed them.'

Luke (18:15-17) uses similar words, with the very striking difference that he uses the Greek word for 'babies' instead of Mark's general word for 'children'. Mark's word for 'children' can be used for children of any age, but the fact that Jesus 'took the children in his arms' seems to say that at least some of them were very young. Luke underlined this:

'People were also bringing babies to Jesus to have him touch them. When the disciples saw this, they rebuked them. But Jesus called the children to come to him and said, "Let the little children come to me, and do not hinder them, for the kingdom of God belongs to such as these. I tell you the truth, anyone who will not receive the kingdom of God like a little child will never enter it."'

Matthew does something very interesting, for his own creative purposes, under the prompting of the Holy Spirit. He records the incident in chapter 19, verses 13 to 15:

'Then little children were brought to Jesus for him to place his hands on them and pray for them. But the disciples rebuked those who brought them. Jesus said, "Let the little children come to me, and do not hinder them, for the kingdom of heaven belongs to such as these." When he had placed his hands on them, he went on his way from there.'

Do you see the bit that is missing? In the chapter before this (18:1-5), Matthew has already used another occasion to challenge adults to 'become like little children':

' At that time the disciples came to Jesus and asked, "Who is the greatest in the kingdom of heaven?" He called a little child and had him stand among them. And he said: "I tell you the truth, unless you change and become like little children, you will never enter the kingdom of heaven. Therefore, whoever humbles himself like this child is the greatest in the kingdom of heaven. And whoever welcomes a little child like this in my name welcomes me."'

It is clear that Jesus used children as visual aids to challenge adults about the kingdom of God. But he also made an important statement about children themselves. He said that the kingdom belongs to them.

Jesus seems to be doing two things at the same time. He challenges adults that they will never find their way into the kingdom of God unless they become childlike. The challenge is also, of course, an invitation: the kingdom of God is given to those adults who can receive it 'like a little child'. At the same time, and on the basis of the challenge to adults about childlikeness, Jesus teaches that children already belong to the kingdom of God. These gospel passages are about both adults and children.

Jesus seems to be saying that the kingdom of God, which adults may never enter, that which they may struggle to enter, already belongs to children. Or, put another way, children are already where adults may end up, if those adults can, by an act of will, become childlike.

That the radical nature of this teaching grabbed the gospel writers is seen by the fact that all three follow their version of Jesus meeting children with the account of a man who could not become childlike. We have come to call him 'the rich young ruler.' His story is in Mark 10:17-27; Luke18: 18-27; Matthew 19:16-26.

Here is an adult who would not let himself be given what he wanted most. He wanted to earn eternal life. He could not become helpless and be given it. Being able to be given something seems to be the essence of childlikeness in the mind of Jesus. It does seem that utter helplessness is the basis for Jesus speaking about the kingdom of God belonging to children.

It is certainly not some 'qualities' of childhood that bring about acceptance with God. Nowhere are we taught the need to become something special before God can accept us. In fact it was this attitude about earning salvation which Jesus most opposed, and which God's gospel of grace confronts - as the 'rich young ruler' discovered, to his great disappointment.

So to argue that children belong to the kingdom of God because they are loving, natural, humble or innocent is to miss the point. In addition, it is to be naïve about children, who are observably not always loving, natural, humble or innocent, a point not lost on Jesus, who was clear-eyed about children, as he was about everything else. (See Luke 7:31-35, where Jesus compares his generation (of adults) to children.)

In traditional Christian circles the idea that adults need to become childlike, utterly helpless, is readily accepted. That sense of helplessness is captured, for instance, in Toplady's old hymn, Rock of Ages.

'Nothing in my hand I bring,
simply to thy cross I cling.

For many adults the challenge to utter helplessness is the final hurdle at which they stumble. The 'rich young ruler' is not the last adult who wanted to do something after being told it had all been done by Jesus. The kingdom of God is entered by grace, received by faith. It is a gift from God, not earned by doing things. See how Paul said this in Ephesians 2:8:

'For it is by grace you have been saved, through faith -and this is not from yourselves, it is the gift of God.'

The young man talked about 'eternal life'; Jesus spoke about 'the kingdom of God'; Paul writes about 'being saved'. Are they all the same thing? Many would say that, if we are talking about adults, whilst they are not exactly the same, each phrase attempts to describe a similar relationship with God.

But as soon as there is a suggestion that there may be an overlap between 'the kingdom of God' and 'being saved', in relation to children, we are in a minefield. If the only basis of salvation is repentance towards God and faith in Jesus Christ, how can this mean anything to an 18-month old child who can't talk yet?

Jesus taught that the kingdom of God belongs to little children. What could he have meant? Let us look at the matter of children and the kingdom of God.

Children and the Kingdom of God

The kingdom of God is at the heart of the message of Jesus Christ. It is also a dominant theme in the Old Testament.

Jesus started his public ministry by announcing the arrival of the kingdom (Mark 1:15). After his death and resurrection, he still emphasised it (Acts 1:3). Paul, the apostle, also 'majored' on the kingdom of God. In Acts 28:31, we leave Paul in a rented house in Rome boldly 'preaching the kingdom of God' and 'teaching about the Lord Jesus Christ'.

Because of this you would think Christians would be fairly clear about the kingdom of God. They aren't. One reason is that the Bible itself presents so many aspects of it, and not all of them fit neatly together, at least on the surface.

So, the kingdom is present, but also future (compare Mark 1:15 with Mark 14:25, for example). Some apparently already possess it (Mark 10:14), but others are outside it (Mark 12:34).

One key to a Christian understanding of the kingdom of God is that Jesus sometimes linked it to himself. See, for example, Luke 11:20, where Jesus is challenged that he can defeat demons only because he is in partnership with the top demon. In reply, Jesus says he overthrows the demonic kingdom because he embodies, in himself, a stronger kingdom: 'If I drive out demons by the finger of God, then the kingdom of God has come to you.'

When Jesus says that the kingdom of God belongs to children, he is saying that children belong to him. What does that mean for children? About which children does he say this? It sounds as if he is saying that all children are in the sphere of God's grace. But don't all people now begin life outside the grace of God (because of sin)? But what does sin mean to a two-year-old?

To see what answers Christians would give to questions like these, I carried out a little research project a while ago. I approached a wide variety of Christian men and women, from different denominations, both clergy and lay people. I outlined the following situation:

'Imagine there are two families, living on either side of you. Each family has a two-year-old child. One set of parents are atheists; the other set are committed Christians. Now imagine that in tragic circumstances both children are killed on the same day, and you are to visit each home. What would you say to each set of parents about their child's destiny and on what grounds would you say it?'

All but one person I interviewed said they would want to say to both sets of parents that their child was with God. One person said he would have to tell the atheist parents their child was in hell and it was their fault! That position follows logically from a very strong belief in the universality of sin, linked to a strong position on the idea that God chooses, or 'elects' some people for salvation, and not others. When taken to the 'edge of logic', it is said that Christ died only for the elect. Fortunately, we do not have to go any further into this here!

So almost all the people said they would say that both children are with God. When asked the basis for saying this, the answers ranged from 'I have no grounds for saying it, but it is what I would want to say' to 'but all children belong to God, so what is the point of the question?'

Most people want to believe little children belong to God, that he looks favourably on them. But this might be sentimentality, not truth. What is the truth about children and God, about children and the kingdom of God? The question can be stated simply, but it is a profound question. And there is a range of answers. I will set out seven answers. Let me say right now that I hold the seventh.

Each answer is held quite sincerely by Christian people. And each answer has a shaping effect on the way those people relate to children in ministry, whether as parents, teachers, pastors or adult friend. Each answer deals with the problem of humanity's rebellion against God.

Answer 1:
All children start life outside the kingdom of God.

This answer assumes that children of all ages are in exactly the same position before God as adults: responsible and accountable, even if they are too young to exercise repentance and faith. It assumes that all the biblical passages about human beings being out of touch with God (for example Genesis 3 and Romans 5) apply equally to children as to adults. The child has been 'caught up' in the rebellion of Adam against God.

The way back to God is through repentance and faith. There are, of course, enormous problems with applying this to very young children. For example, how can we talk about 'repentance and faith' from a child not yet capable of language?

There is also the challenge of what Jesus said about children and the kingdom of God. He said, remember, that 'the kingdom of God belongs to such as these' (Mark 10:14). What he said is there in the text. What it means will need to be thought about carefully. But it cannot be ignored - he did say it.

Much of that thinking will be about 'original sin'. This phrase has become acceptable theological shorthand for humanity's total and ongoing involvement in Adam's rebellion against God

(Genesis 3). If Romans 3:23 teaches that 'all have sinned', this includes every human being, of whatever age, says this answer.

This is such a fundamental matter we need to have some of the discussion right here. The Bible is clear about sin and its consequences. It is also very clear about accountability to God by every person who continues Adam's rebellion. It is the involvement of very young children in that rebellion which is the point of contention.

This issue of sin and its applicability is so important, we need to pause and check something. The fact is that you and I, and every person reading this book, has lined ourselves up with Adam's rebellion. We have all sinned, in thought, word and deed. We have done things, and not done things, which give evidence of this. If we are reading this book, it is not unlikely that we have accepted God's invitation to turn from this rebellion and accept the amnesty God offers because of what Jesus achieved. We are Christian, wonderfully caught up in the forgiveness of sin through Christ.

But each of us had been in need of that forgiveness. Some will have begun their journey in a Christian home. Some began in circumstances far from Christian. However we started, each of us had lined up with Adam's rebellion. Some had actively rebelled. Others had passively drifted from God. The outworking of sin differs in each person's experience: the fact of sin remains.

We have already struggled with this in an earlier chapter. There it was interesting theology. Here we see how it works out in practice. The central issue is: How are children involved in the rebellion of Adam? For some it is quite clear: from conception the child is sinful because the child is human. For others, it is not as clear-cut: there is a bias towards sin, but what if the child is not really aware, or capable of being aware, of this? Is that child accountable before God?

It seems reasonable to say that when a child can have a conscious experience of sin, the child can have a conscious experience of guilt. Before that there is a lack of understanding, and therefore no accountability. Remember that interesting Old Testament teaching about not knowing right from wrong (Deuteronomy 1:38; Isaiah 7:15)?

What, then, is the status of a child before God at the outset of life? This is a central struggle of this book, because so much hangs off the answer. An adequate answer must do justice to two realities at the same time: first, the reality of rebellion and sin; second, the reality of what Jesus taught about children and the kingdom of God.

This first answer puts its weight behind the reality of sin, but it basically ignores what Jesus taught - or sees it as not affecting the application of that reality. All have sinned, including children, in Adam, and that is that.

This first answer has been a strong motivator for a certain kind of evangelism among children. If children, like adults, are in eternal danger apart from repentance and faith, it is a matter of great urgency to give them an opportunity to respond to the grace of God in Christ. Children should be helped, as soon as possible, to make a 'decision for Christ', a phrase which has come to equal 'converted' for many involved in evangelism.

At its best, this answer has motivated people for evangelism. At its worst, it has resulted in children being manipulated towards the responses desired by some adults. Even at its best it has confused children. I have spoken with several adults, and young people, in evangelistic settings, who were confused about themselves and God because they had been manipulated into making a childhood 'decision for Christ'. They had been told they were now Christian, but here they were, convinced they were not and wanting to become one of Christ's followers. We had to undo things first.

One person I spoke with thought he had been 'converted' four times, and was still not sure about God's attitude towards him.

This first answer is usually held by people who care deeply about children, and about what happens to them. But it seems to ignore what Jesus said. Are we really to minister to children of all ages solely on the basis of their rebellion against God?

Answer 2:
The presence of a Christian parent establishes right standing before God.

Answer 1 is about an inherited sinful nature. Answer 2 argues that the presence of at least one Christian parent cancels out the consequences of a child's sinful nature, at least until they are of age to answer for themselves.

So a distinction is made between children, based on their parents. If a child has a Christian parent, that child belongs to God. If neither parent is a Christian, the child does not belong to God.

The thinking behind this answer is based on biblical teaching about the covenant. This is the special agreement made by God with Abraham (Genesis 17), with the people of Israel (Deuteronomy 29) and with the Christian church (1 Peter 2:9 - 10). Those who become part of this special agreement, this covenant, become the people of God. Their children are born into this covenant. So when Paul says in 1 Corinthians 7:14, 'Otherwise your children would be unclean, but as it is they are holy', this is interpreted as teaching that children gain right standing before a holy God because at least one of their parents is a believer.

This answer meets a deeply felt need in Christian parents. Many of them believe their own children start out in life in a special relationship with God, but just as many seem to lack certainty about this belief. I remember attending a special meeting at a conference in New Zealand. The conference was about evangelism among children outside the churches. The meeting had been called to discuss the status of the children of Christian parents. Over half the conference attended. The questions asked indicated that until Christian parents have some peace and certainty about their own children, it is hard for them to think about kids outside their churches.

As an outcome of this answer we might expect to see strategies about urgent evangelism among parents. As each parent is converted, there would be a multiplier effect, as the covenant influence of what has happened spreads out. The fact that this answer has apparently never led to this kind of evangelism shows that it really is an answer to meet a need in Christian parents. It assures these parents that their children have a right standing with God. It is not an adequate answer to the main question about the status of all children with God.

Answer 3:

The presence of a Christian parent creates privilege, not right standing.

This is a 'softer' version of answer 2. It simply says that to grow up in a Christian environment increases the likelihood of eventual Christian discipleship. The child will see Christian values modelled in the home, and will be taught Christian truths. The child will grow in an environment of faith.

It does not follow, automatically, that the child of such an environment will enter into their own faith experience, of course. Ask many Christian parents, caught up in the pain of rebellion against all they hold dear, bewildered by the vehemence of rejection, and riddled with doubts about their role in it all.

So this answer makes no claim about the status of the child

before God. The covenant idea lies behind it , but is applied less rigorously. The child is privileged because of the presence of at least one Christian parent, and a hopeful conclusion is drawn from this situation.

Answer 4:

The experience of baptism establishes right standing before God.

That the child has, or has not, been baptised is what matters to some adults. If the child has been baptised, there is a right status before God. Without baptism, one assumes, Answer 1 applies, that is, that the child is outside the kingdom, cut off from God.

In the majority of churches that take a strong line on the role of baptism for little children, the presence of adult faith, as 'sponsors' of little people who cannot yet speak for themselves, is called for. This takes us back to the covenant idea. The child is caught up in the faith circle of the adult(s), usually the parents.

Historically, especially when many children died in infancy, the drive to baptise them was urgent and sometimes frantic. Obviously if one believes that being baptised is essential to salvation, the idea that little children will go into a 'Christless' eternity without baptism will drive one to baptise as many as possible as quickly as possible.

Today there are an increasing number of parents in churches which baptise infants who are uncomfortable with the idea, or at least with the strength of this answer. It is not unusual to find parents delaying baptism of their babies, especially when this is associated with the idea that the experience will somehow change the actual status of their child with God. 'My child already belongs to God. How dare anyone suggest otherwise?' Such parents are happier with the next answer.

Answer 5:
The experience of baptism strengthens privilege.

This is a 'softer' version of Answer 4. In this answer, baptism, of itself, achieves nothing about status before God. Assuming it is done in the context of faith, the baptism experience enhances the possibility of future personal faith, because it takes place in a Christian environment. Thus this experience is put alongside all the other expressions of faith the child will witness in a Christian home. It will be one of the shaping factors the child will take into account when they decide what they will do about personal faith in Christ.

This brief discussion does not exhaust the issues around infant baptism. But, thankfully, that matter is not central to this book.

Answer 6:
All children belong to God.

This answer seems straightforward. It is clearly the opposite of Answer 1, that is, that all children start life outside the kingdom of God. But what does 'belong' mean, especially in relation to the death of Christ for sin? Is this answer suggesting that little children somehow do not need forgiveness for sin, or that they are not sinful? What looks so simple gets quickly complicated.

For example, W. H. Griffith Thomas, an Anglican theologian of an earlier generation, argued that 'all children are included in the great atoning sacrifice, and belong to Jesus Christ until they deliberately refuse him.' That is, until a child can have a personal experience of sin, and therefore of guilt, the child is covered by Christ's saving work.

But to link the status of all children with Christ's death seems to be talking about salvation. What, then, is the status of the child who later does 'refuse Christ'? Are they then 'unsaved'? There are many adults, including people from strong Christian homes, who are quite definite that they are not Christian. To hold that they belonged to God through Christ's death, but now do not, opens a theological Pandora's box.

There are other people who want to hold that 'all children belong to God' without bothering too much about theology (although, given that theology is 'thinking about God' it is hard to see how this is possible). The answer then becomes a warm, woolly statement with no solid foundation. There is nothing particularly wrong with wanting to 'feel good' about children. But their eternal destiny matters beyond our need for 'warm fuzzies', and if God has said something definite on the matter we need to take heed.

Summary.

Here, then, are six answers to the question about the status of young children before God. Answers 2, 3, 4 and 5 are about children in some kind of Christian context.

Answers 1 and 6 are about all children, and are at loggerheads with each other. One says all children begin outside the kingdom, apart from God. The other says that all children are saved. Are we forced to choose between the two, or is there another option? I think there is. Let us look at a seventh answer.

Children and evangelism

In this chapter we will outline a seventh answer to the question about the status of a child before God. It is based on the idea that all children belong to God, but it also deals with the fact of sin.

Some people fear that if we hold that children begin with God, we have cut the nerve of any need for evangelism among children, because we have eliminated the reality of sin. This is actually an argument wider than simply children. It takes us into the heart of a big missionary debate, about culture and Christ. We need to be aware that passion can run high on this one, so fasten your seat belts! The issue is stated in the following questions:

'Is a culture that has no specific knowledge of Jesus Christ, or of the God of the Bible, therefore 'Godless'?'

To go further:

'Is such a culture, and the people in it, under the sway of satanic influence, given that the choice is either God or Satan?'

When contact is made with people who have no prior Christian understanding this question becomes a burning issue. The question and the answer given to it shape the mind and the strategies of those on mission. This is so whether the location is desert, jungle, high-rise apartments or suburbia.

One of the classic images many Christians carry in their heads about evangelism is the idea of 'bringing Christ to people'. The wording conjures up the image of people without Christ/God before Christians arrive. They will continue without Christ if Christians never arrive, apparently with eternal separation from God the certain outcome. Do we 'bring God' to people, or is

God already ahead of us? There are three published stories that compel us towards the answer that God is ahead of us:

1. Don Richardson in *Peace Child*, (Regal Publications) tells the story of a missionary in despair, until he saw in the culture of a tribe in Papua New Guinea a God-prepared connection as a bridge to the gospel. It is quite a story!

2. J. Donovan in *Christianity Rediscovered*, (SCM Press), tells the story of a Jesuit priest in East Africa who saw that after one hundred years there were no practicing Christians outside the 'ghettos' of Christian hospitals and Christian schools. He got permission to take only the gospel to Masai tribes. He worked on the basis that God was already there, and carefully applied the missionary principles of Roland Allan, a Protestant strategist. The results make breathtaking reading. This is probably one of the most exciting books about careful evangelism ever published.

3. Bruce Olson's story *Bruchko*, (New Wine Press), is about a young American who broke all the rules, followed a strong call from God, and found himself with a Latin American tribe. He stumbled into the principles Donovan had studied, never knowing them as a system, and God mightily used him. On the way, he discovered that God had gone ahead of him into the tribe.

By the way, Don Anderson went on to write *Eternity in their Hearts* (Regal), to challenge anthropologists who claimed missionaries 'mucked up' local culture. This is a live issue today, with strong divisions even in missionary societies about the status of the 'native' culture. Without denying the influence of Satan in cultures, Richardson provides evidence from ancient times, to the 20th Century, of God influencing cultures too.

So you see, any approach to evangelism that is based on the idea that anybody begins with God is going to attract some attention, not all of it friendly. This is equally so even if the subject is children. The seventh answer to the status of the young child before God tries to balance belonging and rebellion.

Answer 7:

A child has a 'belongingness' that may become rebellion.

In many ways we have reached the heart of this book. I am persuaded that the principles outlined in this chapter, and the next, can inform and guide passionate, thoughtful evangelism among children. They can also be of practical worth to pastors and parents in their nurturing role with children.

One does not have to hold a hell-fire and damnation position to be committed to urgent evangelism among children and their families. Love can also be compelling. The eternal destiny of children matters deeply. But too often in evangelism the fear of hell has been made the centre, instead of the love of the Saviour. Paul reminds us that the love of Christ drove his disciples to urgent evangelism (2 Corinthians 5:14).

This seventh answer is that all children begin with God, but will drift from that position unless an effective nurturing or evangelistic influence operates in their lives. It is a belongingness that **may** become rebellion. The desire to nurture that belonging, and to avoid that rebellion, propels us into urgent teaching and evangelism.

There is no assumption that the belonging **will** become rebellion. Full account is taken of humanity's rebellion against God and the child's potential to be part of that rebellion. But that potential is held in tension with Christ's own teaching about children and the kingdom. Taking the child seriously, this answer holds that all children begin with God, but that they will drift from that safe position unless the drift is halted and reversed.

This answer makes sense of the fact that the faith of many adults began with Christian nurture in the home and grew into mature personal Christian discipleship. Some adult Christians have never doubted they belong to God. They have been nurtured in that sense of belonging; they have agreed with it; they have grown in it. Their lapses have been temporary. Then they have owned the faith for themselves, expressing this in some appropriate way - for some in baptism, for some in confirmation, for some becoming a soldier for Christ.

There are some people whose belongingness never became open rebellion. They have never consciously said 'no' to Jesus and they have grown into mature Christian adulthood. It needs to be said that to be held in such a position of belonging and to grow in this to Christian maturity is as much a demonstration of the resurrection power of Christ as any story of rebellion to faith.

It is, of course, possible never to say 'no' to Jesus and not grow into mature Christian faith. Some adults have never consciously rebelled against God. They have simply drifted further and further away, living as if God did not exist. Their rebellion has, in one sense, been a passive one. But whether one has 'spat in God's face', or just ignored him, the rebellion has consequences. Ordinary sin is as deadly as the more dramatic kind. People who indulge in both need to say 'yes' to Jesus.

But 'saying yes' can also have its problems. If there are too many stories of converted drug addicts, prostitutes, sporting stars and beauty queens, the 'ordinary' Christian with no drama in their story begins to die inside. Drama can become the norm for true conversion, and the Christian who has never said 'no' to Jesus begins to wonder if they have ever really said 'yes'.

So being raised in a Christian home can be a danger to your spiritual health! Especially if the family's understanding of conversion to Christ is based solely on a 'moment'. Even Christian parents can be sucked in by this, unless they have confidence in their own child's status with God. Many times I have observed Christian parents become very unsettled about their own children at conferences that are about child evangelism. As I said before, it is hard to plan outreach to other people's children if one is worried about the status of one's own!

Evangelism and nurture.

Some Christian parents have not yet worked out the relationship between nurture and evangelism. This is usually because they simply identify their children with the sin of Adam. On this basis they assume that their children are outside the kingdom until they have made a definite decision to opt into it. I have been present when parents have discussed the status of their children (in their presence once!) thus: 'Johnny is saved; Wendy is close; we are not sure about Fred.' No wonder children get confused!

Another way of stating this seventh answer to the question about children and God is to say that God views each child with favour, and that this favour continues until the child turns their back on it. The image is then of someone facing towards God until they face away from him.

This idea of 'facing towards' and 'facing away from' underlines the fact that a child does not pivot from one position to the other. Any child's turning away will be by degrees, as the child develops (concurrently) a growing understanding of life in relation to God and a capacity to respond to, or rebel against, this understanding. The dynamic journey described in that last sentence applies to all children as they learn about God and grow in their capacity to reflect on life and its meaning.

This means that as children grow older they are in an increasingly demanding situation personally. They move from total dependence on their parents towards direct accountability with God. This idea of 'accountability' has caused some havoc among Christians interested in children's ministry.

The 'age of accountability'

Is there a moment in time, before which a child is not accountable to God, and after which the child is accountable? I believe the answer is a clear no. The idea that there is such a moment has often sidetracked people in their evangelism among children. On the one hand they have pushed too hard for a 'decision', believing this could settle the status question. If a child has said a special prayer they are now right with God. This very static, formulaic description of 'becoming a Christian' should be enough to make us wary. Passionate, dynamic human beings are the subjects under discussion. There will be nothing static about the way such human beings decide about Christ.

Another sidetrack has been to worry too much whether or not any child of any particular age is capable of responding to the gospel. Here the outcome is the opposite to the first sidetrack - here evangelism is slowed, even avoided. And again it is based on a static view of persons. The unique individuality of each person is affirmed strongly by Christians. That should be enough to reject any approach that generalises about children, and puts them in one box. Each child is on a unique human journey. Studies in child growth and development are very important, but they describe the general scene, not any particular child.

That there is a point beyond which a person is directly accountable to God for their attitude and actions seems certain. Jesus said that it is possible to be 'not far from the kingdom' (Mark 12:34). God alone knows when a person crosses over into, or drifts out of, the kingdom. This is a very releasing truth for those of us involved in evangelism, including child evangelism. If

God decides about a child's final accountability, our responsibility has limits. We are called upon to practice responsible evangelism, but we are not held finally responsible for the response which is given.

What is our responsibility in evangelism? 2 Corinthians 4 has some clear principles for us:

* we are to make an 'open statement of the truth' (verse 2)
* we are not to 'distort the word of God' (verse 2)
* we are to display the impact of the message in our lifestyle (verse 5)
* especially in our willingness and ability to serve others (verse 5)

These principles apply equally in evangelism among children. They provide deep challenges to those adults who want to be part of such a ministry. To be able to explain the meaning of the death of Christ to a group of seven-year-olds, without distortion, one must have a very clear and deep understanding of that truth. To serve a group of silly or surly ten-year-olds week after week calls for capacities beyond our ordinary strength. No one ever said ministry with children was the soft option! We need to release our best people into this ministry because so much hangs off it.

As the children grow and develop, they are increasingly accountable to God. We will teach the gospel and nurture the children knowing that belongingness may become rebellion. In the case of children outside the regular influence of Christian modelling and teaching, it is a belongingness that is very likely to become rebellion.

So evangelism must be part of our ministry with children - a thoughtful, careful kind of evangelism that respects the individuality and personhood of each child, yet operates in the urgent context of humanity's broken relationship with God. This respect will keep us from demanding too much from the child. The urgency of the situation will keep us from asking too little from the child. Walking the line between demanding too much and asking too little will take all the Christian maturity we can muster.

Evangelism and education

Christian education and evangelism are locked together. True Christian education and nurture are necessarily evangelistic. Those involved in Christian education must expect, and sometimes call for, a response if they are to be true to themselves, theologically and educationally. Evangelism must be teaching-evangelism, which provides content and a basis for responding. 'Responses to God' created in situations that lack content usually don't last long. As the ordinary demands of life pound away at what people believe, they begin to lose track of why they believed in the first place.

Some people are not happy with the idea of evangelism being so strongly linked to the teaching of children. There will be talk about 'laying good foundations', but again, it is all too static. The question is not whether or not a child can respond to what is being taught. Any human being who receives information responds. They do something with it. They have an attitude towards it. Any teaching we give will be responded to. The question is not whether or not any response is given; the question is what kind of response has been made?

So we need to check the responses being made, not to brainwash, but to help us understand what we have communicated. One Sunday School lesson I spent a deal of time retelling the story of Jesus curing a leper. I invited the children to draw a picture about it. I was surprised to see one child drawing an animal with spots on it. I was told that this was the leopard Jesus cured! My poor diction had created the wrong image, and this had controlled the response. In a few minutes we had corrected the error, and the response was corrected too.

As to the kind of response being given, this is a little harder to determine in a group. Often a child seems to be simply adding to their pool of Bible knowledge, and people assume this is a good thing. But children never simply add to knowledge. They form opinions about, and attitudes towards, what they learn. One series of lessons in an RE class I taught seemed to be building an image of Jesus as Superman. He moved into situation after situation and 'fixed' it. Apart from there being no tension (he always won without any struggle), there was a degree of unreality about it all.

So I took a lesson on prayer, and introduced the children to some people I knew, through books they had written. Two involved illness that had been cured through a mixture of care and prayer. Two involved situations (death and Downs syndrome), which had not changed despite much prayer. We decided that Jesus was not just 'magic', and that there were a few puzzles in life with God. We recognised that he could help people go on in tough situations. I thought this was not a bad investment in the future lives of those eight-year-olds!

What kind of evangelism?

This chapter outlines a seventh answer to the question about the status of a young child before God, and the implications for ministry with children. It is being argued that all children begin with God, holding this in tension with the reality of humanity's rebellion against God. So far we have established that the nerve of evangelism is not cut by maintaining that all children begin with God. So what is affected?

What changes is the style and stance of evangelism. It affects what we do and how we do it. It even affects what we say. One experienced child evangelist has said that the question to ask children is not 'Have you ever said "yes" to Jesus?', but 'Have you ever said "no" to Jesus?' Behind these apparently simple differences there are two very different theologies, each with practical implications for ministry with children. One way to sharpen the discussion even further is to talk about children and conversion. We turn to that topic next.

Children and conversion

What is Christian conversion? In essence, it is to make a radical break with the past, and to reorient one's life around Jesus as Lord of life. Two ingredients are essential: a radical break; a new lifestyle. The acid test is not about the words we use, it is about the life we lead. As Jesus himself said in Matthew 7:21

'Not everyone who says to me, "Lord, Lord" will enter the kingdom of heaven, but only he who does the will of my Father in heaven.'

Leading a life that is pleasing to Jesus, including the rejection of those things that he would be displeased with, has application to a person of any age. It is a little difficult, however, to think what a 'radical break with the past' might mean for a four-year-old. I mean, when I became serious about Christian things at 20, there were a number of matters to do with my past and my lifestyle that needed attention. The challenge to a radical break made sense to me. Even someone brought up in a Christian home (as I was not), who has a strong encounter with Christ, knows that the Christian knowledge they have needs to be brought more clearly under the Lordship of Christ.

But what past has a four-year-old to break away from? Given what we know about the need of children of this age to think about things in 'concrete' terms, it will not be very helpful to speak to them about 'sin' in the abstract. But if we want to make 'sin' concrete, we are in danger of providing long lists of bad behaviours, then thinking we have dealt with 'sin'. All we have done is provide a list of sins, that is, of some of the ways sin expresses itself in practice.

What is it that God calls us to repent of? It is our fundamental rebellion to the idea that God should rule - in our life and in this world. Is not sin the refusal to let God be God - in our life or in the world? That rebellion will express itself in many ways, but the list of ways is not sin. Rather, the list is simply that - a list of sins. Sin expresses itself in sins. We call on people to repent of the rebellion which is sin. We are interested in people dropping habits and actions that are 'sinful', but we know this needs to be an outcome of conversion. The desire to get rid of behaviour that displeases Jesus, and the power to do so, is one clear sign that a person is converted.

Another clear, and accompanying, sign of conversion is that a person keeps on getting rid of, or refusing, actions that displease Jesus. According to Jesus, the test is not starting in a race, but finishing it (Mark 13:13). Does this mean we can't be sure about our salvation? Yes we can, because the ongoing desire to please Jesus in all we do, and the impact this keeps making on the way we live our life, is a clear indication to us that we belong to God.

Back to our four-year-old. What is it that we want to say to him/her about themselves and God? The answer to that depends a lot on how we think about evangelism, and conversion. And those answers depend on what we think about children and the kingdom of God.

There are two quite different approaches, both of which come from the study of missionary work in other cultures. The first is the 'boxed set' understanding, which looks like this:

THE BOXED SET

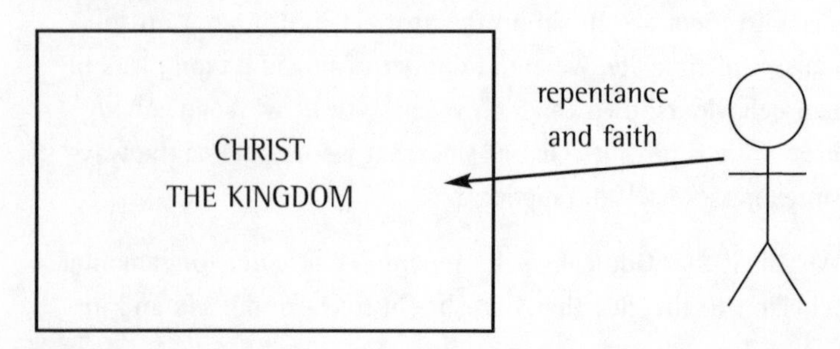

In this diagram, the person is outside Christ, or God's kingdom, or salvation. That is their starting-point. By repentance and faith, the person moves from outside to be inside. In Christian terms, they are then 'in Christ'. Before that, they were outside of Christ and justly condemned by a holy God.

This approach has some strengths and some weaknesses:

STRENGTHS

(a) there is an emphasis on a 'moment,' which could be very helpful in a person's sense of assurance.

(b) there is a clear line between being in God's kingdom and being outside.

(c) the approach would very easily fit with a sense of urgency, and may even generate it.

(d) there are a number of Bible verses which apparently support this understanding, for example John 3:16 and other verses about being born again.

(e) one would think a person would know if they had taken this step.

WEAKNESSES

(a) the very strong emphasis on a 'moment' has meant that many people deny the reality of their other experiences with God. There may have been many 'moments'.

(b) there are a number of Bible verses which apparently support this understanding, for example, Acts 16:14 and others which emphasise movement towards.

(c) the approach is static, and does not cope with those who say they have had the experience described, and even helped others find Christ, but are now themselves atheist. I know people who say this.

(d) push the approach too hard, and we are left with too

strong an emphasis on what the human agent has done, that is, we have 'salvation by works', the works being my decision.

The other approach to conversion has been called 'the centred set', and looks like this:

THE CENTRED SET

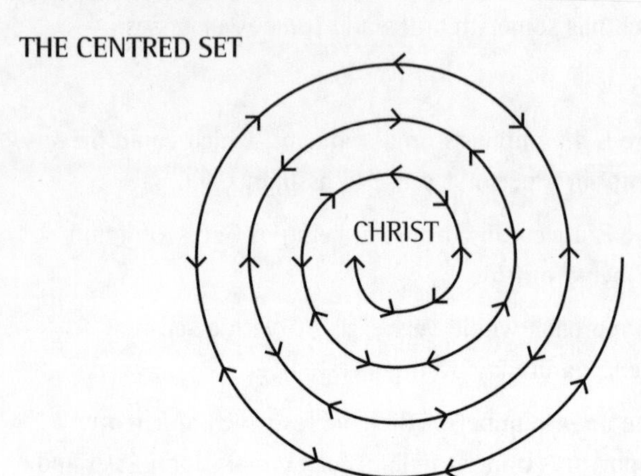

In this diagram Christ is in the centre, just as he is in the 'boxed set'. The concentric circle is portraying the idea that every person in the world is moving towards or away from Jesus at any moment in time. A person may not know Christ, but be moving towards him. Another person may be a Christian, but at this moment is moving away from him. It is possible to be a disobedient Christian.

This understanding, too, has some strengths and some weaknesses:

STRENGTHS

(a) this is a dynamic diagram, which seems true to the human experience, that is, that we move around in our relationship to things spiritual.

(b) there is an emphasis on grace, even though it is quite possible to keep walking away from Jesus. There is not the same sense of a barrier as in the other set.

WEAKNESSES

(a) if things are really so open-ended all the time, how does a person ever become sure of anything? Especially, how can anyone be sure of their salvation?

(b) there is, for some, a feeling that this approach may be saying that everyone will be 'saved', or at least that no one will be lost. (This is known as 'universalism'.)

(c) because this looks so open and friendly, some are concerned that sin may be being treated too lightly.

So, what does one do when faced with this kind of choice? These diagrams depict at least two of the main ways we can think about people, God and conversion. How do we choose between them? Do we have to choose between them?

One of life's great discoveries is 'both/and'. So many important things in life are presented to us as 'either/or' choices. Here is another example. Do we have to choose between the 'boxed set' and the 'centred set'? Both have strengths, and both have weaknesses. How do we choose? Here is a good example of a time we need to take the 'both/and' approach. If we do, the diagram now looks like this:

THE COMBINED SET

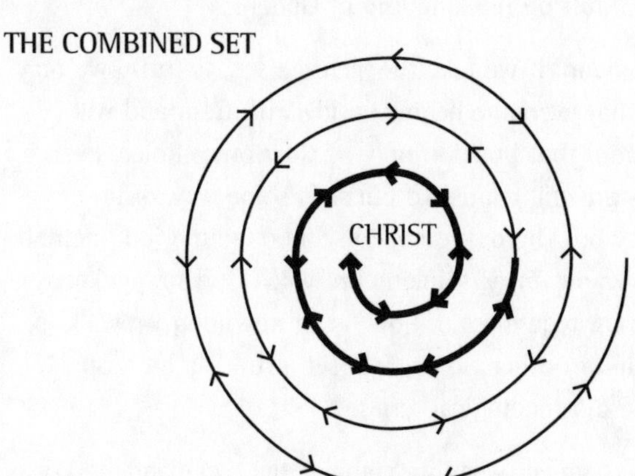

What this is showing is that all people move backwards and forwards in their relationship with Christ. It is also showing that the idea of being in or out of God's kingdom also can become a reality. At some point, known only to God, a person can move into the situation in which they are now growing or drifting from Christian discipleship. They have a relationship with Christ as Lord, different from the relationship they had with him before. Before it was a creature/creator relationship, based on the grace of the creator. Now it is a child/parent relationship, based on being adopted into the family of God through a faith-link to Jesus the Christ.

Now take all of this back to our four-year-old. Remember, this is why this chapter was written! If we take the 'boxed set' as truth, the response of the child, as with a person of any age, is everything. If the child will repent and believe, they will be saved, and will move from outside God's kingdom into a relationship with Christ. Because the response is everything, we will be very urgent about it. We may even, in our sense of urgency, 'push' a little. Until the child has 'accepted Christ' they are justly condemned by a holy God. That condemnation comes out of the idea that every human being has been caught up in the rebellion of Adam. So every human being begins life offside with God and outside the kingdom of God.

On the other hand, if we take the 'centred set' as truth, we may want to say that everyone begins onside with God, and will move away from that position only by their own choice. Even if they do, they are still related to Christ in some way, distant though it may be. The desire not to seem or sound judgmental may lead to 'warm fuzzy' thinking, in which God simply keeps on accepting us, regardless of how far or how long we walk away from him. In other words, this 'set' sounds a bit suspect, 'liberal' in the old theological terms.

But look what happens when we combine the two diagrams. We now have the dynamism, but we also have a definite relationship with Christ, a relationship that has a beginning and needs to be developed. At some point a person moves into a different kind of relationship with Christ. This may not be one point in time. It may be a period of days, weeks or even months. **It is all about direction.**

Only God knows when that new relationship, that new status, has come into being. But it has to happen if we are ever going to talk about 'being Christian' in a way that means something specific. Then we are talking about growth or drift in Christian discipleship. We are not just talking about a nearness or 'farness' from the grace of God, as wonderful as that idea is for all humanity.

Now here is the important bit for our four-year-old (they won't go away, will they!). Every move towards Christ can be described as a 'decision towards Christ'. People don't just drift into a saving relationship with God in Christ. It involves decision, but it may, probably does, involve a number of decisions. And we want to affirm every one of them.

We want to be able to say to every person, of any age, who has made a decision of some kind that brings them closer to Jesus, that what they have done is a good thing. We want to encourage them to keep on going. That may mean we are encouraging more movement towards the point at which they enter into discipleship. It may mean we are encouraging someone who is on the very edge of that relationship. Only God knows.

If we are always positive (and we can be with this 'both/and' approach), we are helping the child (or a person of any age) to keep moving in their journey with Christ. We can affirm what has happened, without claiming too much for it. I mean, if a person has been told that they have just become a Christian, it implies that they weren't a moment before. Which can be pretty confusing for someone who grew up in a Christian home and has loved Jesus all their life. Or for someone who made a 'decision' last year and was told the same thing, that is, that they had just become a Christian. Given that God alone knows when a person 'crosses the line', I am staggered at how easily some people take upon themselves to tell others whether or not they are Christians.

The biggest problem with the 'boxed set' is that it doesn't handle the fact that many people make many 'decisions towards Christ'. If we are locked into the idea that a person is either offside or onside with Christ, we can only talk about them being a Christian or not being a Christian. So, if someone makes a 'decision' that is sincere, deep and strong, we are forced to say that they have become a Christian through that decision. But if they were told the same thing last month by another person, confusion enters. Were they a real Christian before, or not? Some terrible things come out of this box!

It is very releasing to combine these two ideas, when thinking about evangelism. But when we want to think especially about children, we have another matter to consider as well. What is the relationship of the young child to the kingdom of God, from the outset? Notice how we keep coming back to this matter of status before God at the beginning of life. It is fundamental. We have considered this in some detail, and seen that there is integrity in the position that a child begins with God. The intriguing phrase 'decisions towards Christ' calls out for our attention now.

Decisions towards Christ

One of the challenges in writing about evangelism among children is that many adults believe evangelism will be exactly the same for all ages. I have no problem with this idea, as long as the discussion is about the content of the gospel and the lifestyle of the gospeller. But too often 'evangelism' is linked to a particular understanding of response about which I do have some problems.

A particular interpretation of Paul's experience on the road to Damascus, recorded in Acts 9, has been the basis for the dominant understanding of what 'response to the gospel' means in many Christian circles. It has been developed as a 'model' of response. Then it has become something like a goal for the evangelist, who will look for this kind of response, and only this kind of response.

The main ingredients, according to the interpretation, are that the response was sudden, time specific and definite (even spectacular). Paul encountered a bright light, fell from his horse, met the risen Christ and was struck blind. Forever afterwards Paul could point to this moment of surrender to Christ.

This was when Paul made his 'decision for Christ', although this is not a phrase Paul ever used. That phrase has come, over time, to equal 'conversion' in the minds of some Christians, so that response cards at evangelistic events have often referred to three possible categories of response:

(a) decision for Christ.

(b) assurance of salvation.

(c) rededication.

Some see Paul's experience as based on Jesus' own teaching about the need to be born again (John 3), and draw the conclusion that every person must make a clear, time specific 'decision for Christ.' They apply this conclusion to all age groups, including children. The aim in evangelism becomes to help people, of all ages, make a 'decision for Christ', which is equated with conversion.

Now it should be clear by now that I am totally positive about the idea of response. But there are some real problems associated with this use of one interpretation of Paul's experience. For example, the impression is given that this is when Paul encountered Christ for the first time. But this is the man who held the coats of those who stoned Stephen, and heard the martyr's plea that those killing him be forgiven (Acts 7:60). That experience went into the mind of someone already zealous for God, to the point of persecution. The Paul who encountered Jesus on the road to Damascus at noon that day was already on another kind of journey.

Then there is Acts 16. There are two conversion stories in that chapter. One is the Philippian jailer, who as far as we can tell was pagan one minute and Christian the next, with an earthquake in the middle. Very time specific! But in the same chapter is Lydia. She is a 'God-fearer', a term describing a non-Jew attracted to belief in one God. Lydia went to the river with some other women that Sabbath and heard Paul talk about Jesus. During this time 'the Lord opened her heart' and she became a follower of Jesus. A 'sunrise' conversion: Lydia had been moving towards this 'moment' for some time. Forever after, Lydia would certainly point to that morning as significant. But she had been on a journey for some time, and had made a number of decisions about faith before that morning.

Many people, including children, make 'decisions towards Christ'. Let me tell you a story that illustrates how this idea can release us. One night I was at an adult evangelistic event, as a 'counsellor'. When the invitation was given, I went out alongside a young man, to be available to him when appropriate.

When we got to talk, I asked the series of questions I use in such situations. First, 'Why have you come forward?' The answers I have received over the years have ranged from 'To become a Christian'; to 'To go to the loo' and 'To see Billy Graham up close'. To the last two I asked a follow up question like, 'Was there any other reason?' The answer, in both cases was 'No', so I directed one to the loo and the other one back to his seat. This is a very important first question!

This young man said, 'To become a Christian.' So my next question was, 'Have you ever done anything like this before?' He replied, 'Yes, three times.' To which I asked, 'What happened those times?' He responded, 'I was told I became a Christian.' 'Did it work?' I asked. 'No' he said. 'Well, how do you know it will work this time?' 'I don't. I just hope it does.' My response card allowed for 'conversion', 'assurance' and 'rededication'.

What emerged was that he had been told three times he had been converted, based on a 'decision for Christ'. What further emerged was that, like many of us, he wanted Jesus to be his Saviour, but not his Lord. There were areas of his life, getting smaller as God worked on him (!) that he wanted to keep to himself, while benefiting from God's forgiveness in Christ.

After talking, I suggested that what he had done this night is make another 'decision towards Christ', like the ones he had made before. I encouraged him to keep on going. We had talked about Christ as the master of the life and lifestyle of his followers. He would continue in the local church he had joined and to read his Bible. And I would wish response cards had at least one other category!

Rather than making a once-for-all decision to follow Christ, many people take gradual steps into the dawning light that can become the radical reorientation that is Christian conversion. It is not necessarily a cumulative process. Only God knows the point at which a person is 'saved'. Remember the 'boxed sets' and the 'centred sets'?

If we faithfully teach what it means to belong to Christ, and the cost, we are evangelising. This is true, whether it is our own children, or outreach ministry. Children can, and probably will, make decisions towards Christ as a result of our teaching. It may be appropriate to understand what their response means for them, but we are not responsible to get the response, or to decide what it means to God. That is incredibly releasing.

Certainly people who say they 'belong to Christ' should be able to say something about their decision-making process, and even its timing. But, as one writer put it, it really doesn't matter if you spin around quickly on one heel, or turn slowly and thoughtfully. What matters is the direction you finally face, and that you walk in that direction.

Many people grow into faith. They move through steps and stages at their own pace. This is partly because of their own unique developmental clock, and partly as a result of their (unique) experiences of life. The joy of Christian ministry is to be available to people, helping in the arena of knowledge and the interpretation of life in relation to God.

The children of believers are not unlikely to mirror something of the experience of Timothy in the New Testament. 'From infancy you have known the Holy Scriptures, which are able to make you wise for salvation through faith in Christ Jesus,' wrote Paul in 2 Timothy 3:15. Even here there are no pressure-free guarantees given. The 'Timothys' of this world are in touch with the knowledge that can lead to salvation, but they must still exercise individual faith to enter into what is promised.

The Christian life is an ongoing series of responses to Christ. That doesn't mean we are converted over and over again. But it does mean that we continually give evidence about the direction of our life by the decisions we keep on making. As we move through the ages and stages of life we will face many decisions. We give evidence of the direction of our faith journey by the decisions we make along the way.

For example, it is not possible for a nine-year-old boy to submit his sexuality to Jesus. His sexuality is dormant at that age. By the time he is nineteen, with hormones hopping in all directions, it is important that this aspect of who he is has been related to Christian discipleship. Similarly, an eighteen-year-old single woman cannot surrender her marriage to Jesus, except in some theoretical, 'in principle' way. Not that there is anything fundamentally wrong with 'in principle' submission. It is just that it will have to become reality for a 28-year-old mum if Christian discipleship is to be real. Finally, we can only actually surrender to Christ those things about which we face real choice.

What the idea of surrender means for a Christian will change beyond recognition between the ages of seven and seventy. It is the direction of the decision-making that decides the destiny. Jesus taught that it is not about 'blasting out of the blocks', that matters most; it is finishing (Matthew 10:22). The Christian life is more like a marathon than a sprint. (See Hebrews 12:1-2.)

The children with whom we minister will make any number of decisions towards Christ. When we accept this, and understand what is going on, we can be positive, supportive of the child and settled in our own mind. Calmly urgent, in fact.

Children and the Holy Spirit

Do you think children can be Christians? It is highly likely that someone reading this book will answer 'yes' to that question. If your answer is 'yes', there are several other matters that come on line immediately, not least issues to do with the Holy Spirit and children.

I make the following assumptions, having taken the position that children can be Christians, that is, born again of the Spirit of God, determined to live in ways that please their Lord Jesus:

(a) Children who are Christians are able to call God 'Abba/Father' through the work of the Holy Spirit who indwells them (Romans 8:15).

(b) Children who are Christians will have assurance of their salvation through the inner testimony of the Holy Spirit (Romans 8:16)

(c) The desire of children to call Jesus 'Lord' is the outcome of the work of the Holy Spirit in them (1 Corinthians 12:3).

(d) Children who are Christians are candidates for the fruit of the Spirit (Galatians 5:22).

(e) Children who are Christians are candidates for the gifts of the Spirit (1 Corinthians 12:4-11).

My observation is that we were probably doing all right until point (e). Some may have found it a bit startling to even have any list that speaks of the Holy Spirit and children. We have to move beyond that attitude, if we do believe that children can be Christians, because one of the defining characteristics of a Christian is that the Holy Spirit lives in them (points a and b above).

Many will not be bothered about (a); (b); or (c): but they will pause at (d), and they will be bothered about (e). Once the matter is raised, I find that most adults agree that the Spirit will produce his fruit, in some form, in the lives of children who are Christian disciples. But they will often balk at the idea of the Spirit's gifts being displayed through children.

The first, big, issue here is the application of any biblical truth to children. This was focused for me in an interesting way at the beginning of 1988. The Lausanne movement and the World Evangelical Fellowship were co-sponsoring an international conference on the subject 'Conversion'. It was to be held in Hong Kong, over four days, and would involve 'evangelical scholars and leaders from all parts of the world'.

I wrote to the organizers, asking if they were planning to include a consideration of children and conversion, given that children made up nearly one-third of the planet's population. The reply was that they had forgotten to include any specific focus on children and conversion, and included an invitation to prepare a paper and present it at the conference!

Dr Jim Packer chaired the conference, and the other participants were a 'who's who' of the evangelical world. It was a privilege to be there. Papers had been read before we arrived, so each presenter was given 15 minutes to summarise their paper, then answer questions for another 15 minutes. We all took part in the general discussion, which followed. Everyone present had produced a paper, so the first two days was given over to 'tuning in' to each other. Then began the discussion, as we tried to see what conversion might mean in the late 20th Century, in the light of biblical principles.

Early in the discussion phase, I had cause to question an assumption that appeared to be evident in many presentations. It was that biblical passages applied, with no concessions, to children just as they did to adults. I questioned that assumption several times on the first day, and then again on the morning of the second day. Jim Packer, seeing me move forward during the first discussion after lunch, said, 'All right, Ron, we must not assume that this passage applies to children without any qualification or adjustment!' He continued to acknowledge the point as the conference went on.

When the draft of the conference communiqué was distributed on the last morning, I read it with a sinking feeling. There was no mention of children in the text, at all! I thought I had failed completely until I saw a special PS, which acknowledged that the application of the agreed principles to work with children raised special questions that needed more attention. Children, it appeared, were on the global agenda.

The point of dialogue at the conference in Hong Kong was whether or not the Bible is, first of all, a book for adults, and about adults. The answer seemed to be 'yes'. This does not mean that Bible teaching is not applicable to children, but it does mean that the teaching needs to be applied to children in ways that take into account the fact that they are children.

This book has already done this several times, for example, in the matter of sin. When Romans 3:23, 'All have sinned and come short of the glory of God', is quoted as if it has universal application to all humanity, including babies, there is a problem. We have noted teaching like Deuteronomy 1:39, about little children 'who do not know the good from the bad.' We have noted Jesus' teaching about children and God's kingdom. There is enough in the Bible itself to cause us to pause, even before we bring to bear the insights of developmental studies. They alert us to some of the boundaries on children's thinking as they develop.

Back to the Holy Spirit and children. There are passages that teach that every Christian is involved in the work of the Spirit: we have quoted several already. Do these passages apply to children without any adjustment, or qualification? Of course not! One has to be consistent, at least. But, they do apply in some way. The fact that application to children will need some careful attention, and that the application of adult-related teaching will not be one-to-one from adult to child, does not mean that there is no application to children.

So the bottom line is that if we believe children can be Christians, we are driven to the conclusion that they will be involved with the Holy Spirit in some way. My own observation is that many adults, having drawn the conclusion as a general principle, are more comfortable talking about the fruit of the Spirit in relation to children, than they are talking about the gifts of the Spirit.

It would be possible, of course, to eliminate the gifts of the Spirit in relation to children altogether, by holding that they would be inapplicable developmentally. It would be interesting to hear those who took this position say when a person does become a candidate for the gifts of the Spirit. At what age? We have already seen in this book that individual differences between children make any generalisations about them relatively useless (which means that they are also relatively useful!) If we are committed to excellence in ministry with children we will hold very carefully to the idea of the uniqueness of each child.

Which means we will seek to identify principles that have universal application, but then we will apply them individually. No 'all 10-year-olds' from us! In this chapter we have identified several universal principles about the Holy Spirit. The application of those principles to children will challenge us in new ways, but there will be an application to children. To eliminate that application without any other discussion says more about the adults doing the elimination than it does about the principles.

Some adults are wary, even a bit scared, about gifts of the Spirit. They have seen, or they have heard about, some 'odd' activities associated with those gifts. The 'edge' of the Pentecostal movement does have some unusual activities. People in the mainstream churches, even those touched by 'renewal' often look aghast at Pentecostal church activities (or at least their reported activities).

As with all caricatures, there is an element of truth in the reactions. One has only to check early morning TV to witness activities done in the name of the Holy Spirit that are often unusual to say the least. Seeing people fall backwards at the touch of someone in the 'name of Jesus' can be disturbing, especially when it is then associated with teaching that claims this is to be the norm for Christian worship. Healings, deliverances, prophesies: all are a challenge when adults are the focus. The idea that these things can and perhaps should manifest themselves in our children's church every week goes beyond 'challenge' to become challengeable.

The choice need not be between unquestioned acceptance of the application of 'Holy Spirit teaching' to children and total rejection of the idea. The fact is that such teaching, in relation to all Christians, is there in the Bible. That its first application is to adults seems to be established. That it also has application to child disciples of Jesus seems equally sure. So, what is a way forward?

Some argue that we are simply to introduce children to teaching about the role and gifts of the Spirit, then trust God not to let it get out of hand. Whilst that sounds very spiritual, it ignores every useful insight from child development studies. Of course, those who hold such a position usually don't think child developmental studies have anything to do with a work of God! They may argue that those studies deflect us from being open to all that God would do in the lives of children.

Few hold such a strong position. Many walk the difficult line between:

* not wanting to see children manipulated, emotionally or spiritually
* not wanting children to miss out on all that God has for them.

Some who have thought deeply about these matters finally 'land' on the cautious side, based on careful theological and developmental study. One such is Francis Bridger, in the 2000 edition of *Children Finding Faith* published by Scripture Union.

Bridger argues for the introduction of the 'less dramatic' spiritual gifts to children. By these he means things like generosity and compassion. He thinks the more spectacular gifts, like tongues, healings and prophecy might not be appropriate for children. He points out, very helpfully, that the gifts of the Spirit in the New Testament are not personal gifts; they are for the church. The gifts are given to build up the church (1 Corinthians 14:12). Gifts must be evaluated by others in the church (1 Corinthians 14:29). The gifts of the Spirit are not personal toys, to take home and play with. They are given to the church to help its members grow in the things of God.

On the other hand, maybe gifts of the Spirit, in relation to children, are meant to be 'taken home', in the sense that the family is the setting for much of a child's spiritual development, especially when they are younger. In a home of Christian disciples we would expect to see practiced both the fruit and the gifts of the Spirit. In the close and caring atmosphere of a Christian home, the child could be introduced to the gifts, with very careful attention to their individual capacities. After all, the family is a 'church' for the child. It is where two or three are gathered together in the name of Christ, and he has made promises about being there when that happens. We often will refer to a local church as a 'family'. More precisely it perhaps should be a 'family of families'.

Bridger rightly wants us to take careful note of what comes from child development studies that 'ring true' to what we see in children. He starts from the assumption that 'all truth is, finally, God's truth'. If we agree with that idea, we will include in our ministry with children anything that helps us be with children in ways that will avoid them being manipulated, or scarred.

I agree with Bridger about not manipulating children. There is such a thing as 'spiritual abuse'. But I know other careful people involved in ministry with children who testify to seeing God work amongst children through some of the more spectacular gifts of the Spirit. One of these people is Alan Price, a Church Army (Anglican) captain who has ministered with children over many years in England and other countries. His workbook is called *Children in Renewal*, published by Kevin Mayhew in 2000.

The corrective that Alan employs in ministry situations is to maintain a high ratio of adults to children. That is a very strong corrective. When lots of children are exposed to excitement and suggestion, with little adult 'filtering', things can go wrong. And the 'adult filtering' needs to be of the highest quality. Once again, work with children demands the best we have. Immature adults will do as much harm amongst children as poor ratios! Which takes us back to the family setting: the place where the ratio of child to adults is usually a very good one!

Some adults will say that this whole discussion is all too hard. If we have to walk around so carefully, why not simply stay away from the territory? Well, it all depends what you believe about children and the Holy Spirit, doesn't it? This chapter will end on this open-ended note, because the subject remains firmly on the current agenda. Anyone committed to excellence in ministry with children will keep prayerfully working on it.

Children and the church

He approached me during a break at a conference. I knew he was involved in a medium sized church in a large country town.

'Could you consider doing a consultation with our church on its ministry with children? We are particularly concerned that there won't be a church in the future unless we start getting more children and families into our fellowship.'

'Talk to me about the situation. An outside consultant might be the last thing you want. You might be able to do the work yourselves.'

'Really? We would need something to help us get started. And I am not sure we have the expertise to carry it off.'

'Well, you obviously are a bit passionate about it. Are there any others like you?'

'I suppose there are, now I come to think about it. Three, possibly four people would share my concern about children in our church.'

'That's great, and certainly enough to get going. I'd suggest you might use this strategy planning sheet to find out where you are, and work out a way ahead.' (Note: A copy of the suggested strategy planning sheet appears on pages 94-95 of this book)

'So, we would keep going down a line until we answer 'no'?'

'That's right. I have to warn you that this is a deceptively simple tool. It asks all the right questions, and it assumes someone is the 'champion' of the process.'

'Champion? That's a strange word to use.'

Outreach to Children and Families

Strategy Planning Sheet

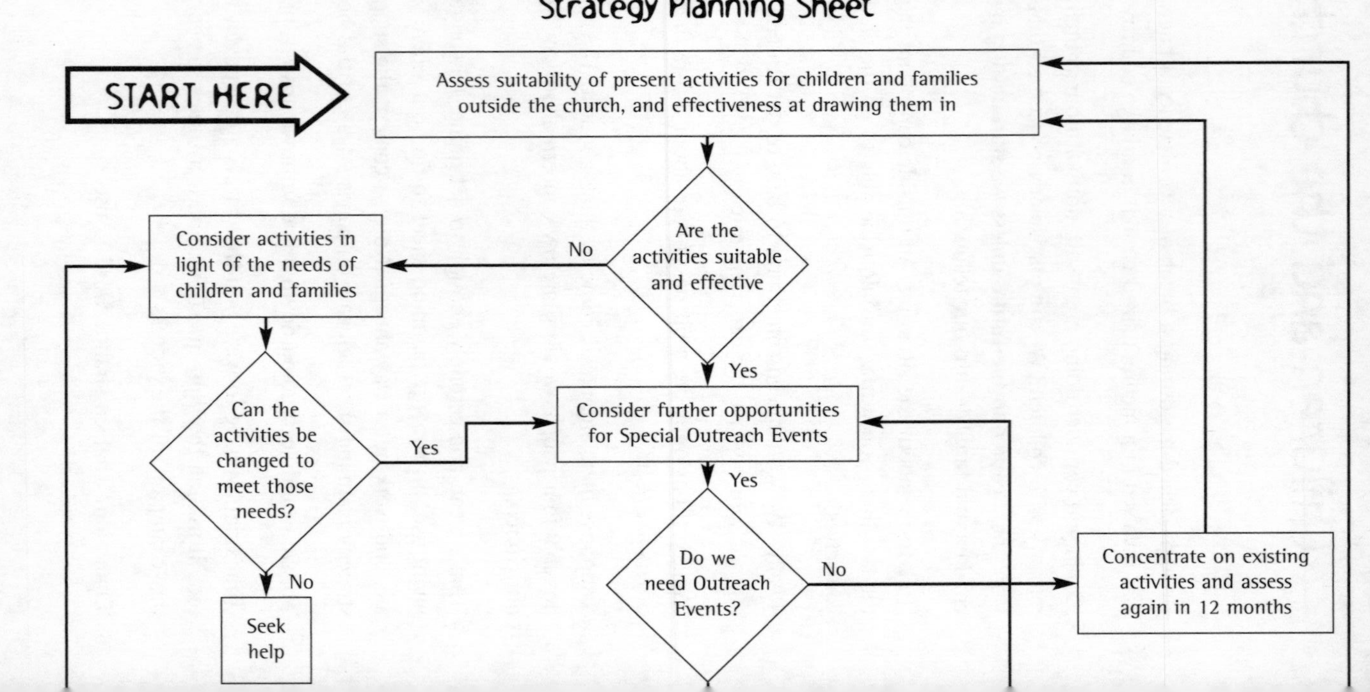

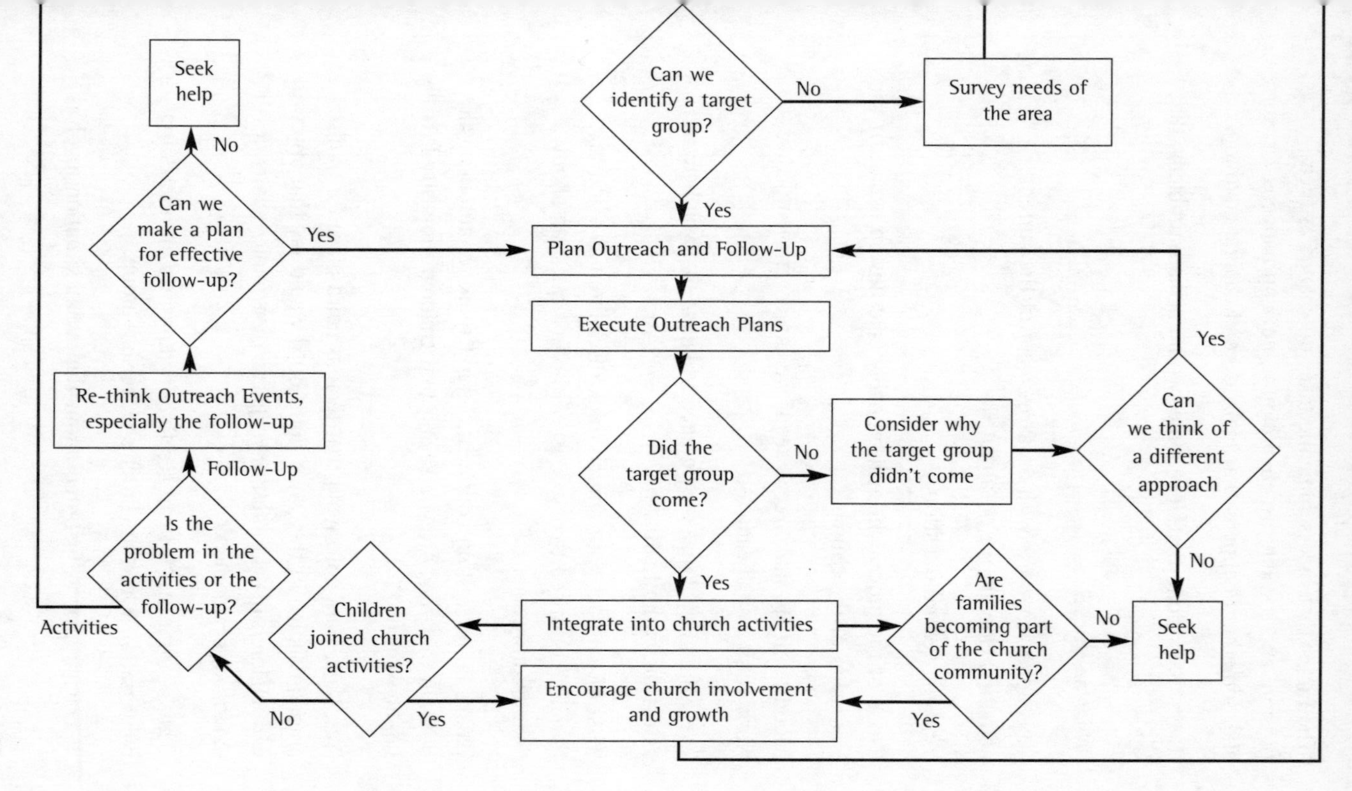
Can we identify a target group?
No
Survey needs of the area
Yes
Plan Outreach and Follow-Up
Execute Outreach Plans
Did the target group come?
No
Consider why the target group didn't come
Can we think of a different approach
Yes
No
Seek help
Yes
Integrate into church activities
Are families becoming part of the church community?
No
Seek help
Yes
Encourage church involvement and growth
Children joined church activities?
Yes
No
Is the problem in the activities or the follow-up?
Activities
Follow-Up
Re-think Outreach Events, especially the follow-up
Can we make a plan for effective follow-up?
Yes
No
Seek help

'The fact is that unless someone takes on change as their passion, and is willing to champion it, nothing happens. Or worse still, something happens that really doesn't change anything.'

'Been there, done that! There are two immediate problems that I see.'

'What are they?'

'This approach starts with an assessment of the current activities. How do we go about that?'

'And the second question?'

'None of the group who will probably take this up is part of the leadership of the church.'

'Good points to make. Let's see if we can cover them as we work out a way ahead.'

'Well, fire away. What do we need to know, that will help us assess the current situation?'

'First of all, does your church think of children as being in families? I noticed that you asked the first question about children only.'

'That's an interesting comment. I don't think we automatically think in that way. Are you saying that children's ministry is really family ministry?'

'Yes, I am. I am not saying that there is not a place for ministry among children in their own right. But I would say that any work with children that ignores, or neglects, their family-relatedness is damaged, or doomed.'

'That's strong stuff. I can see that leading into an interesting conversation with the church's leadership group.'

'It usually does. A first step about the overall situation involves paper. You need to get hold of copies of anything the church has in writing about its mission, its values and its ministries. Including, of course, anything about children or families. Do you reckon such things exist?'

'Some do, although I am not sure how long ago some of them were done. I think that is one of our challenges. The community around us has changed, and I don't think we have carefully looked at things for a while.'

'It might be better for the church to produce a current mission statement about its whole vision.'

'In terms of mission statements, we produced one two years ago. Is that current enough?'

'Only just, I would guess. Your area is changing fairly rapidly. It would be good to check the appropriate printouts from the latest National Church Life Survey. I assume your congregation took part in it?'

'Oh, yes. But we have not been sure about how to best use the data that came back to us. It sounds like this will help us do that. But why is all this stuff necessary, if we are talking about children in church?'

'Any consideration of children and church services will raise the bigger questions about ministry with children and their families generally. Outreach programs, community-related programs, parenting programs, school-based programs... they all become part of the discussion.'

'Why?'

'Because I assume your church wants to be around and functioning in 30 years time?'

'Sure. So?'

'So unless you do some creative outreach and community connecting, you probably won't be.'

'Ouch! Yes, we are dropping numbers and drifting a bit. So, you are arguing that researching our context will need to be part of the process?'

'Yes, it will. And because your church is in an area that was included in some of the Australian Bureau of Statistics work, you can buy a report that will give you some important insights into the wider community.'

'That sounds good. What comes next?'

'I'd suggest that you need to survey your congregation about everything that goes on that has anything to do with children and families.'

'Could you help design a simple questionnaire we could use?'

'Sure. But don't depend only on paper. One of the good things about doing your own survey is that your team knows the people. Follow up the questionnaire with conversation. Get people to talk about their dreams.'

'By the time we had done all that, we would have a fair idea of the mood of our church, I would think.'

'You sure would. Then you can take on the clients of your ministries.'

'What do you mean, 'clients'?'

'I just mean the people with whom ministry is carried out. Parents of children in programs, for instance.'

'So, the process needs to be wider than the leadership of the church?'

'Yes. The leadership contact is crucial, of course. But if we never ask our clients we will never find out how our current ministries are being received. And we may well miss the boat for the future.'

'I'm not sure I know what you mean. Can you give me an example?'

'Sure. Say we are about to renew the contract of a staff person with responsibility for family ministry. Would you not think it fundamental that we check with parents about their experience with the person?'

'Sure.'

'Well, I have to tell you that it doesn't always happen. Perhaps it is surprising, but I keep hearing about reappointments without consultation with those with whom a person is in direct ministry.'

'Are you saying that lots of people should not have been reappointed?'

'Not really. I am simply illustrating a principle. We must consult with the recipients of ministry, not just with the givers of it, or with those who supervise them.'

'It is an interesting point. Some of our elders have been saying that we perhaps should consult with those who don't come to our programs. What do you think? Is that possible?'

'Certainly it is possible, and I am delighted it is already 'on the table'. As I understand it, your church membership is mostly people who drive to it, rather than who live around it?'

'There are some who live nearby, but generally you are right.'

'Well, you could letterbox the area, with a communication that says you are wanting to be a church that can make a positive contribution to families around you, asking people to fill in a simple form and return it in a self-addressed envelope. You would invite people to include their name and address, letting them know that you will invite them to a "search meeting".'

'Does that work?'

'You won't get hundreds, if that is what you mean. But you will get some. And they are 'gold' to you, if you listen well. You won't change everything because of the comments of a few local people, but you would be foolish to completely ignore them.'

'OK, so now we have all this material, and we have listened to lots of people. What now?'

'Now you need have face-to-face consultation with the leadership team. I have assumed that the whole process would be endorsed by the leadership.'

'Oh, yes. We would be foolish to undertake such a process without at least their endorsement in principle.'

'I agree completely. What you might like to do in preparation for the meeting of your team with the leadership group is to let me have a look at your report in draft form. It sometimes is useful to have someone from "outside" comment.'

'That is a generous offer, which we will probably take up. If we think it is needed, could you possibly be open to meeting with the leadership group, alongside my team?'

'You mean, as a kind of consultant?'

'Yes! That is where we started this conversation, isn't it!'

'It is, but where we are now is much healthier than simply bringing in an 'expert' from outside to do all the research work, don't you think?'

'I do. We have a lot of work to do locally, but I am excited about the possibilities.'

'I am too. I will pray for you as you get started. Perhaps we could exchange email messages as you go along?'

'That would be great. Can we finish this conversation with some ideas about the meeting with the leadership team? In fact, I would be most helped if you could describe what you do when you meet with leadership groups as a consultant.'

'Ok.'

'How do you start such a meeting?'

'Usually there is no question about children "belonging" to the church. It's that word "belong" that I get into the conversation early.'

'Because then I ask what was done last Sunday to let the children know that they belong.'

'Wow! That is being a bit blunt.'

'Maybe, but that's what it comes down to, doesn't it? We can talk forever about belonging in theory, but what finally matters is what happens in practice. I am not suggesting you go down this line. I am telling you what I do as a consultant. As someone from outside, I can ask tough questions. They don't have to face me the next week!'

'I can see that mixing local homework with a consultant might push things along. But surely the question about "belonging" applies to all the different groups in a church - teens, singles, grandparents, more?'

'Of course, and the same kind of question can be asked about any of them! The question is a good one, for any group within the local Christian community.'

'Does this mean that you would arguing that the services revolve around children?'

'Not at all. That is the fear of some leaders; that the church service will be turned into a "circus", or at least that children will be placed on a pedestal.'

'And this is not so?'

'Certainly not. The point is to argue that children be included in some ways, most of which are simple.'

'Like?'

'Acknowledging birthdays, a 'kidspot' 'in the service, a soft toy section for littlies...it goes on and on. There is no shortage of tried ideas around, but they need to be tailored to each situation.'

'I think some of our leadership will still be nervous about the church services becoming childish.'

'I'm sure you are right about that fear. The aim would be to help them think about services becoming childlike - simple, straightforward and focused. If the needs of children are being met most congregations find, often to their surprise, that adult enjoyment and participation rises too.'

'Is that because what children need adults want?'

'Precisely! It doesn't mean things fall away, even intellectually. The presence of children, taken seriously, makes preachers and service leaders work harder at their vocabulary, for instance. And simpler words means all ages understand better, not just children.'

'So, looking at children in the church helps the whole church?'

'It sure does.'

'I am really excited about all of this. I can't wait to get home and get a team together.'

'Great. But first we have a session to attend at this conference, and it is just starting.'

Starting out

This chapter illustrates a theme of this book, that is, that what we do in practice demonstrates what we believe in principle. A theological centre of this book is that what we believe about the status before God of a young child controls how we treat that child in ministry.

This connection between principles and practice is also shown when we publish for children. Let me demonstrate this by looking at *Starting Out*, a Scripture Union booklet for primary-age children.

In 1987 SU Australia first published *Starting Out*. It is still in print, having been revised in 1999. The booklet aims to help children over seven years old to 'grow as a friend and follower of Jesus'. I was part of the team that put the first edition together.

When anyone publishes, there is a public declaration of principles made. *Starting Out* is no exception. It bristles with declared principles. We will look at three of them, because they have permeated this book too.

That each child is unique sounds simple, but it is a profound statement if it is followed through in practice. One of the sadder aspects of our society is to see how much we talk about the worth of each individual, but how much we treat people in categories.

There is a category 'children', but it is made up of individuals, each one unique and special. You only have to speak to parents who have more than one child to find out that each child is different. 'How can the same couple produce such different people!'

Page 3 of *Starting Out* looks like this and shows right at the beginning that we are serious about individual differences.

Whatever your interest in ministry with children, whether as a parent, a teacher or a friend, all of the children you care about are on their own, unique, journey with Christ. One clear

principle underlying *Starting Out* is that a first step in ministry is to listen, before we talk.

One of the least helpful and unbalanced images about evangelism and teaching is that we are only called on to tell people something, to proclaim the gospel. There is a time and a place for proclamation, as there is for telling. But before we tell someone what we want to say, it might be useful to find out what they think, or know. This is no less important in ministry with children.

Some adults have become hardened towards what they think is the gospel because of their experiences as children. They were badgered about sin and about behaviour. Sin and behaviour are important matters, but it is God who really matters. Look at Kate, Chris, Daniel and Sophie on pages 4 and 5.

Kate is on a journey of discovery. She knows some things and is open to finding out lots more. She is not ready to decide about Jesus. We will respect that she is not ready for any kind of final decision. We will, under God, add to the pool of knowledge Kate has, so she will have a good basis for decision making when she

is ready. We will want Kate to know that making a decision about Jesus is important, but we will avoid pressuring her into something for which she is not yet ready.

Chris is on a different journey. It includes discovery, but he already knows a great deal. Probably brought up in a Christian home, he thinks of himself, rightly, as a follower of Jesus. He wants to know more about what that means in practice.

We will want to affirm what Chris has experienced so far, and we will welcome his desire to 'go on'. It is really very exciting, isn't it! So, the idea of affirming what is already there is very important. Too often, people involved in evangelism spend the first contact with people like Chris 'straightening out' some of their 'errors'. The trouble is, an 'error' is too often something that does not fit into the preconceived ideas of the evangelist!

With children like Chris it is important to stay positive. He is likely to be full of biblical facts, to know a lot about Jesus and other biblical people. He is also likely not to have thought much about what it might mean to the way he lives. That is, he will be like a lot of adult church-goers!

So our priority is to build on his desire to find out more about following Jesus. We can help him go behind the biblical text, assisting him to ask why things happen, or are said that way. With Chris the challenge is not simply more Bible knowledge, more facts, but the introduction of 'so what?' questions about the knowledge he already has. Handled well, Chris will surge forward in Christian discipleship. He represents a very different starting point compared with Kate.

Daniel begins somewhere in between the first two children. He is like Kate in wanting to be sure. He is like Chris in wanting to know more about following Jesus. But he does not have Chris's basic Bible knowledge. So our conversations with Daniel will need to go along a different route. We will want to assist his need to become sure. But we know there are biblical truths he needs to encounter, and to absorb, if this is to become his own assurance.

That is, it is relatively simple to tell people about assurance. It is a little more challenging, but longer lasting, to arm them with the truths that will undergird their own assurance. We want people to be assured about their faith because God gives them that gift, not because we said it.

So the journey with Daniel is an interesting one, different to the others. To treat Daniel like Chris, or even like Kate, would be to fail in our commitment to the individuality of each child.

Because Sophie is different again. She does not know much, but is open to finding out more. How does she begin? Pause and ponder your answer to that question. What would you say to an eight-year-old child who asks how they are to begin the journey of being a follower of Jesus?

Too often some adults push too hard at such a moment. For the child it starts to feel like an exam, or it sounds like an obstacle course, as Bible reading, church going, prayer, witness, and anything else thought edifying and helpful are piled on to the child. It can all become just too hard.

Sophie needs gentle encouragement to go forward. She knows she needs more knowledge, so the idea of reading the Bible and thinking about what she discovers will be welcomed. She would respond to the idea of some help to do this, either through a booklet or with a person. We want her to go on her own journey of discovery with Jesus. So we will encourage and guide, not simply tell and correct.

Four friends. They could all be in the same class at school. There are lots of things they share about their lives. But each is a unique individual. We will be aware of some of the characteristics of the age they are. But we will be controlled by the idea of individual differences. We are in the people business, not working on an assembly line. This commitment makes all ministries, not least ministry with children, demanding and wearing. We refuse to take 'short cuts' in our ministry with children.

Following the pattern of Jesus, we will meet and deal with each person, whatever their age, as a unique individual. Faced with a child who is responding in some way to Jesus, we could show them this page from *Starting Out* and ask them which child they are most like. The answer will guide our next response. That is why pages 4 and 5 were written!

At the end of *Starting Out* there is another key principle, which is important to this book too.

One day I had a phone call from a friend who conducts adult evangelistic campaigns. 'We are getting lots of children responding at our meetings.' he said, 'Does that surprise you?' I told him that it did not. I said that in a society drifting further and further away from biblical literacy, I would expect children to be fascinated, even intrigued, by Jesus.

'Well, whatever the reason, we are not currently geared to counsel children. So here is a question. I'm about to train a group of counsellors and want to include something about children. If you had five minutes with a child who has come forward at a crusade meeting, what would you want to say to them? We must be realistic - five minutes only, probably with the parents waiting. What would you say? I'll ring back in ten minutes.'

When he rang back I outlined pages 8 and 9 of *Starting Out* which appear on these pages.

I said, 'I would want to say to the child "You are special" and "God welcomes you"'. 'What about sin?' he asked. 'If I had five minutes, with the probability that I might not see the child again, I would want to stay totally positive. I would want to leave the way open for what was said to be built on by the next adult contact. If I try to introduce sin in these circumstances, it would be too much, and may close the door, rather than leave it open. I would want what I did in that five minutes to be part of a journey to faith.'

'That's great,' was the response. I have no idea what he said to those counsellors! But here is a principle being worked out in practice. It is not just about 'being positive', although that is part of it. After all, some evangelistic approaches say, 'We have good news for you - you are a sinner going to hell!' It makes one wonder what bad news might be if this is the good news!

We expressed this theologically on pages 14 and 15 of *Starting Out*, which look like this

When we talk with people, of any age, about how to begin following Jesus, we can begin either with God, or with ourselves. They are both legitimate starting points. If we begin with humanity (ourselves) we will start with sin. If we begin with God we will start with grace. I believe we need to start with grace, for at least two reasons.

First, because God does. 'God is love' (1 John 4:8). Now I know that is not all there is to know about the character of God, but that he is love is foundational. Even God's response to sin comes out of grace. He could have left us to wallow in the outcome of our rebellion. He did not. Why not? Because of his grace, the outworking of his love.

So my first reason for starting with grace is because of God. The second reason is because of us. Behind all the noise and bravado of modern people there is a cry to matter, to be loved. Really loved, not the fairy floss that pop songs produce. In a society so big on self-esteem many people are 'walking wounded'. The only thing they are sure about is that they

don't matter much, not in any way that makes any real difference.

People long for some good news. That God loves them is good news. Their rebellion against God is something that will have to come up at some point. But why start with it? The outcome of 'fire and brimstone' evangelism continues to be stunted people. They are usually so afraid of putting a foot wrong they rarely do anything adventurous, and they don't smile much. On the other hand, Christians are meant to be 'seriously happy people', caught up in the wonder of serving a God who is love, who is himself characterised by grace.

Here, then, are three principles expressed in *Starting Out*, which also are foundational to this book:

1. **Each person is an individual, and this idea will control the way we work with them.**
2. **We can be positive without denying biblical truth.**
3. **We will begin with God, who is love, and therefore we will begin with grace.**

Sin cannot be ignored, of course. As you have seen in this book, it is not ignored in ministry with children, but it is not the controlling reality. Grace is.

PART 2

Putting it all into Practice

20 principles that lead to excellence.

Seeking after excellence

In this final section, we will identify and briefly explore 20 principles that will assist anyone who wants to seek after excellence in their ministry with children. In keeping with the philosophy of the whole book, each principle leads into practice, and shapes that practice.

This section provides a summary of the main thrust of this book. It also provides an 'instant training program', as each segment can lead out into broader issues.

1. We will treat each child as a unique individual.

That every child is unique would seem to be beyond question. Parents often are amazed that two people can produce such different individuals, as they parent their children. We can see our own good qualities, but we wonder where those other things came from!

Our society is built on the idea of the worth of each individual. We make much of this idea, and we even give evidence of it from time to time, especially when disaster strikes. We will spend mountains of money, and enormous energy, as a society, to rescue one person.

But, too often, we place people in 'boxes', rather than see individuals. 'Men', 'women', 'teenagers', 'aboriginals', 'ethnics', 'wogs', 'Catholics', 'fundamentalists', 'homosexuals', 'generation Xers', 'New Agers', 'Westies' ... so it goes on. Once someone has been labelled, we too often relate to the label, not to the person.

I remember being at a seminar during a World Council of Churches conference in Canberra several years ago. The seminar was on relations between men and women in the church. Shortly after it started, it became very plain that those on the all-female panel were all against men, who were the enemy. Especially men who were white, Anglo-Saxon and over 40, of which I was one!

What followed were a string of generalisations about men, many of which did not apply to me and, from the body language of the few men present, was objected to by them too. It was an uncomfortable time. When I attempted to say something to a woman at the end of the session, she said that now I might know better how it feels to be in the minority. I did not take the comment well at the time, but later acknowledged its impact. It was a great learning experience, but it was also a bad example of labelling and its results.

There are many books in print about child development. Many training times will include a session on 'ages and stages of development'. You will have gathered from this book that I want to be careful about this material. My point is that there is actually no child alive who is exactly like any of the 'age and stage' descriptions. By definition, such generalisations describe broad characteristics, not real children.

If we are not careful, we will box children into the generalisations, then not relate to the real children in front of us. Because we are aware of this danger, we will take the time, and make the effort, to 'tune into' the life of each child we have the privilege of being in ministry with.

This is not easy in practice, once we are in group situations. I don't find this easy in RE classes of 30 primary aged children. It is hard enough learning and remembering the names of children you see once a week, let alone recalling individual characteristics! But if we are serious about this principle of uniqueness, we will work hard at relating one to one.

If we have opportunities for evangelism with groups of children, we will plan very carefully what happens after any invitation for response. We will look more fully at response in the next section, but here let us note that each response will be unique. So we will not try to 'counsel' any more than one child at a time. If this means delay, so be it. Better a child be treated in their uniqueness than we 'process' children in the name of ministry.

2. We will delight in every response a child makes.

The question is not, 'Can a child respond to the gospel?' but 'What does a child's response mean?' We will want to affirm every response made by a child to God, and build on it as part of that child's unique journey of faith.

An idea central to this book has been 'decisions towards Christ'. The thinking behind this phrase has been spelt out in some detail earlier. Here let us think a bit more about how it works out in practice.

Sometimes we will be working with children a long way from any clear ideas about God, or Jesus. In many primary RE classes, we will have children for whom 'Jesus' is a swear word only. I have been amazed, and delighted (usually in that order!) as children give evidence that they know none of the stories Jesus told, then become entranced by them. When Jesus is presented to such children, slowly and carefully, he intrigues them. On the other hand, when he comes across as some kind of 'Superman' who never failed, they get bored.

If a child is starting this far back, their responses will be many and they will be usually tiny steps forward. The move into a positive attitude towards RE as a subject might take weeks. That attitudinal move/response is crucial if the child is to be open to listening positively to material about God.

As I write this, we have just finished a series with 9 and 10 year olds in RE, around the theme 'God's good idea'. We explored creation, community, choosing, ecology, death, divorce, and anger. Then, on the final day we explored laughter and fun, as part of God's good idea. As we told jokes and heard about King David dancing before God, I saw some children make some responses towards a more positive attitude. That will take us a step forward for the start of the next series. I will be able to build on that response from those children.

There are others in these classes who cannot get enough about God. Some know a lot about God already. They race ahead in the material, and are in danger of becoming bored, as I plod along with those who need to get to the point of just listening when 'God' is the subject. With the 'racers' my goal is to puzzle them, with 'why' questions. They know a lot about 'what' happened in the stories and incidents we explore, so I throw out 'why' questions from time to time.

We also look at paradox regularly, by asking questions that have 'both/and' answers. One of these is 'It was God's good idea that we care for the environment. Do we care? Do we not care?' The answer, we discovered to both these questions, was 'Yes!' This allowed us, once again, to think about the idea that God planned that people would have choice, so we can choose to follow God's good ideas, or we can choose to go against them.

As we seek to delight in each response given, we face again the challenge to treat each child as an individual. In any class/group situation, we are operating at any number of levels at the one time. We are responding to the child who is losing interest; we are responding to the child who has already done the next three tasks; we are responding to the child whose English is weak; we are responding to the child talking to their neighbour- and that is across one row!

This is why we have to be well prepared. Unless we know exactly where we are going, we will be controlled by the chaos of trying to operate individually with children. The paradox is that it is easier to 'get away with it' if we see children only in groups, than it is to teach children as individuals. But we are not in the business of 'getting away with it'; we are committed to excellence in ministry with children.

3. We will teach so that no unlearning is needed.

One potentially bad application of the 'ages and stages' approach is to limit our teaching to what we think a child of any particular age/stage can cope with. It is breathtaking that we would think we can decide such things, especially if we subscribe to the idea of the uniqueness of each child.

At its worst, the kind of thinking that goes with this could lead to teaching something that we later have to tell children was wrong, or at least not fully correct. One trivial example is to lead children on in their belief in the 'Tooth Fairy', then tell them at some later time it was not true. 'Santa Claus' is, of course, another example.

Why not treat it all as a great joke from the outset, as something we all know is pretend, but we all enjoy pretending that it isn't? Then it becomes a piece of family fun. The other approach can lead to the development of mistrust: if we lied about this, what else have we lied about? If that sounds too heavy, listen to some adults talk about when they began to lose trust.

Then there are Bible stories. In any curriculum that is put together well, the same Bible stories will come up at different stages in the curriculum. They will be handled differently each time, as the designers try to take into account the broader truth in the outcomes of child development studies. In this book, we are not denying that the capacity of children to think grows, only that we take care not to 'lock' children into some kind of cage, based on our understanding about limits.

For instance, if I was facing a class of 13-year-olds for the first time, I would probably open my Bible at the start of Mark 2, the account of the man lowered through the roof on a stretcher. I would do so, if these were 'church' kids, knowing that if they have been involved in Sunday School, they have had this story before, maybe twice.

I would tell them that I am delighted to have them as my class at the age they are, because they can now do things with the Bible they could not easily handle before. We would read the passage (Mark 2:1-12) and I would draw attention to what is said about, and by, Jesus. I would especially draw attention to the statement by those opposed to Jesus, that 'only God can forgive sin', noting that Jesus had just said to the paralytic, 'Your sins are forgiven'.

We would then note very carefully the question Jesus asked: 'Is it easier to forgive sin, or to say "Take up your bed and walk"?' I would slow the class down, and ask which is easier in the situation in the passage, then ask them to vote, allowing a 'don't know' vote.

We would eventually agree that forgiving sin is actually the harder to do. But we would then discover that in the situation described it was easier to say 'Your sins are forgiven', because there was no evidence needed. Whereas if Jesus said, 'Get up and walk', and the man cannot get up, Jesus is immediately discredited. So, in the situation, as described, it would be seen as harder to say 'Get up and walk'.

Jesus knows this is how his opponents are thinking, so he says, 'To show you I can do what is really the harder thing, I say to this man, "Get up and walk"'. The man gets up, showing the opponents that Jesus is capable of forgiving sin, based on their way of reasoning. Jesus, as he does so often, pins his opponents to the floor by taking their position and pushing it to its illogical conclusion.

I would say to the group that this was always happening in this passage, alongside all the true things they have learned about this story before. They are now capable of seeing this deeper stuff, and I am looking forward to 'revisiting' lots of the Bible with them, building on what has been seen before.

In this way, we can build on earlier learning, affirm it, and then move on with the children into new levels of understanding. We can introduce younger teens into a way of thinking about the Bible that they can take into adulthood. This is one reason, by the way, why we need to work very hard at holding onto kids as they move into adolescence. So often, we lose kids just at the point they are capable of really getting into the paradoxes, and the layered complexity, of the Bible.

4. We will not demand too much from a child.

In evangelistic ministry with children, the adults who demand too much from children are those who have one set way of operating. There are a number of booklets available for use with children. Starting Out which we reviewed in some detail earlier, has the strength that it allows the child to guide the adult into an appropriate starting point.

Many booklets that say they are designed to help children in their response to Jesus control the response. Many adults use them because they agree with the approach, based as it is on there being one (only) appropriate response to the gospel. The problem is that too many of the helps produced are based on a formula response, some variation of 'give your heart to Jesus'.

Now, there is nothing wrong with a child thoughtfully 'giving their heart to Jesus', if they know this is a metaphor and have some understanding about what it points to. But for this to be the only response 'allowed' from the child is demanding too much.

We need to move into an era in which adults who are committed to evangelistic ministry with children are chosen on the basis of their maturity in the faith, demonstrated by flexibility, not rigidity, of thought. Given that ministry is with people, and given their uniqueness, plus the multiplicity of responses this leads to, we need adults who can be relaxed in God, committed to finding out what the starting point for the child is. The adult needs to know what resources are available to help the child in their response, and prayerfully use the appropriate one, or none, as the case may be.

We also need to release into ministry with children adults who can be urgent and patient at the same time. Urgency is not only demonstrated by making appeals all the time. And patience does not mean we will never call for a verdict about what is known, or presented. 'Calm urgency' is well aware of the seriousness of what is undertaken in evangelistic ministry. In fact, it is the attitude that takes evangelism most seriously, in the light of the character of God, and of his gospel.

5. We will not expect too little from the child.

If we are determined not to demand too much from a child, we will be equally committed to the idea of not underestimating them. For too long, too many in Christian circles have underestimated what children are capable of, in relation to God.

Children have a sense of 'God' from an early age. We don't have to introduce 'God' questions into the mind of a little child. Some parents with no faith of their own, and with a highly developed sense of fairness, work on the idea that they will allow their child(ren) to hear about God later in primary school, as a contribution to their child's total development.

Few such parents make it beyond kindergarten before 'God' questions come! I have talked to such parents over the years. One assumed that their child had been introduced to 'God-stuff by someone, but could not understand when this might have happened, given the age of the child, and the parents' control of the little one's daily life. We left the conversation with the troubling (to the parent) thought that maybe the 'God-stuff was part of the child's innate makeup: that is, no one need have introduced anything from 'outside'.

There is enough research done by now to allow us to say that children have an inbuilt spirituality. As a Christian, I believe this to be part of what it means to be made in the image of God. We are designed for a link with God, and however much humanity's rebellion against God has twisted that design, it lingers on in us. In little children it lingers strongly. There is evidence that being 'hammered' by the combination of our society's attitudes, and by same-age friends also affected by those attitudes, leads to the weakening of spirituality. [Those interested in exploring this in detail could check out The Spirit of the Child, by David Hay, published by Harper Collins in 1998].

So, one side of not expecting too little from children is based on the capacity of children. The other side of this principle is the challenge to the adult involved in ministry with children, to include some kind of opportunity for the child to respond to the gospel.

I mean, what is the aim of our ministry with children? Is it not that children will be able to make their own decisions about Christian discipleship? Our personal dream is that children will choose Jesus Christ as their Lord, and that they will grow into a deeper and deeper understanding of this commitment. I have carefully called this a personal 'dream', not an aim, because if this becomes our aim in ministry with children, we open ourselves up to the kind of pressure that can lead to manipulation. If we are 'failing' to achieve our aim, we will feel that pressure.

The desire not to be involved in manipulation has led some towards not expecting enough from children. I have felt this pressure, having been appalled by the activities of some adults in their evangelism amongst children. I have seen every trick used, ranging from emotional 'blackmail' to bribery, to get children to 'say the prayer'. I have walked out on some meetings. I have been physically ill after watching some at work. With every bit of grace I can muster, I can (just) allow the idea that such adults may be motivated by some kind of understanding of the child and eternity. But what I have seen too often, has not been love in action; it has been close to 'scalp hunting.'

Resisting the temptation to 'ride that hobby horse' any further, the point here is that seeing children being manipulated by adults led to a period during which I held back from inviting responses from children. I still taught with enthusiasm, and I still prayed towards their discipleship to Jesus. I just didn't want them to be reborn prematurely!

Then I realised two things. Firstly, 'being reborn' is something God brings about, in his own time with each individual. It was the height of human pride for me to think I could decide if and when a child could enter into Christian experience. Secondly, each child is responding each time. That is, we do not control the idea of response from a child. My responsibility is not to decide whether or not a response will be made: it is to check what response has been made. Every presentation of Christian truth will be responded to: for me to eliminate the challenge to respond is actually nonsense.

Of course, the challenge might be a 'little' one, depending on where the children are in their understanding of Christian things. I have never called for a response of 'commitment to Jesus' in an RE class: to do so would break the contract under which RE takes place in State schools; but it would also be too general in such a setting, with children at such very different understandings about, and attitudes towards, Jesus.

But I regularly call for a response to the material we have dealt with in class. We often talk about making choices, and I regularly make the point that I am not there to make them believe what I believe, rather to help them get the facts upon which they can make up their own minds. I know, of course, that every time I make such a statement, there is a definite pressure to decide something. That's fine, as long as I don't press for a certain response, or even for some kind of outward response right then: there is nothing immoral about reminding children that they are choosing beings, and that there are some things worth choosing about!

Here, then is a balance in excellent children's ministry: on the one hand we will not demand too much from children: on the other hand, we will not expect too little from children. Ministry that walks between these two 'boundaries' will respect the children and the work of the Holy Spirit, at the same time.

6. We will see each child as 'family-related.'

In this book it has been assumed that we define little children in relation to the web of relationships that is 'family'. It needs to be said, again, that 'family' is shorthand for all the different types of family around today; including nuclear, extended, blended, institutional, foster, and others.

The very young child, showing that combination of toughness and vulnerability that is uniquely human, needs the physical and emotional support of family to survive. Even as the child develops to the point of comparative, and growing, independence, that web of relationships remains very significant. Of course, for different children it remains significant for different lengths of time.

For no one does family ever become insignificant. Even those who no longer 'have' a family live their lives in the light of that reality. Every Christmas we are reminded of this, as suicides and depressive episodes mount as the festive season approaches. The great time for family, each year, reminds many about what they are missing. Each year it becomes too much for some. Family continues to influence us all our lives. For many, perhaps most, that influence is, on balance, a positive one.

Back to children. In ministry with children we will want to endorse, and enhance, positive family influences in the life of children. It needs to be said that if our contacts with some families show up influences that are not positive, we may find ourselves in an advocacy role. That is, if we take our ministry seriously and have a holistic approach, we may have to do something about an unjust situation. We will, if we are pursuing excellence in that ministry. We will, of course, need to do this with great care.

To be involved in children's ministry is, therefore, to be in family ministry; the two are locked together. What does this mean in practice? At a simple level, it means I will acknowledge birthdays of the children in my ministry, because they are significant to them, and give me legitimate contact with their families. It means that when a child is absent for a period, I will make contact with the family. It means I will plan activities for families from time to time. At another level, it means I will include some kind of planned visitation scheme in my ministry. To do this I will need to make ministry with children some kind of priority. Such a ministry cannot be done with excellence if it is just 'fitted in'.

When I make contact with parents and caregivers, I will have a 'bottom line' outcome in mind. My contacts will include parents who are delighted to see me, and who see me as a partner with them in the spiritual formation of their child(ren). Some contacts may include the opposite attitude: parents who are not happy about my involvement with their child, especially in a Christian teaching context. This attitude is more likely in an outreach situation, but is more and more common in our increasingly multicultural society. A child from a Muslim home, caught up in our program through friends, may begin to show great interest in Jesus. The parents may not be overjoyed at the idea. Then there are the indifferent parents and caregivers, who tolerate what we are doing, until their child starts to show real interest in the gospel. Then 'fanatic' starts to be heard, and pressure mounts for the child to withdraw from the program.

What is our 'bottom line" with the last two sets of parents, the hostile and the indifferent? The bottom line goal is that we will be able to stay in contact with the child. So we will not engage in 'heavy' theological discussions with the parents. We will emphasise the eagerness of the child to learn more about Jesus, and our desire to stay in touch with their child, as a friend. We will assume that the parents want the best for their child, including the freedom to make up their own mind about God. We may actually say that to the parents, if it seems appropriate. I have found it to be appropriate several times. We will emphasise that it is also our desire that the child make up their own mind, in their own time. We will make sure the parents understand that we are not involved in 'pushy evangelism', and that we want to be the most help to their family we can be.

We will seek permission to stay in touch with the child, if it is a situation that means contact will be broken, for example, a holiday mission. Asking permission to write to the child, and letting the parents know that we are happy for them to see what is written, has broken the impasse several times. That we are willing for parents to see what we write to their child removes one of their greatest fears.

Contacts with potentially hostile, or indifferent, families need to go slowly. Ministry with excellence can be urgent and relaxed at the same time. We are not in the business of driving wedges between children and their families. Some quote Matthew 10:34-37 to justify this attitude. In this passage, Jesus says, amongst other things, 'Do not suppose that I have come to bring peace on earth.... For I have come to turn a man against his father.... A man's enemies will be members of his own household... Anyone who loves his father or mother more than me is not worthy of me.' Now, whatever else is going on here, it is not using the Bible well to make this passage the basis for a ministry with children that sets out to antagonize families! Jesus is talking about something hard and painful, the kind of careful commitment that is made in the face of known cost. Deciding that my choice of Jesus as Lord must place my love and loyalty towards my parents in second place is quite different to justifying a ministry based on antagonism.

Having said that, let us balance things a bit. It is too easy to assume we are 'for' the family, in some kind of blind way that will not criticise that family. Someone has written about 'the idolatry of the family' in some western countries. 'Family' is not the controlling reality in God's economy: God's Kingdom is.

The same passage we have just quoted shows this. Matthew 10: 37 says quite clearly, 'Anyone who loves his father or mother more than me is not worthy of me.' And in Mark 3:31-35, when Jesus is alerted to the fact that his family wanted to see him, Jesus said 'Who is my mother? Who are my brothers? Look! Here are my mother and brothers! Whoever does what God wants him to do is my brother, my sister, my mother.'

Jesus was not rejecting his family here, but he was relativising them, that is, making them second in importance. He is showing, in his own relationships, what he later taught, that Kingdom relationships are to take first place, not the family.

In our ministry with children we will work out this teaching very carefully. It is not for us to decide if and/or when a child (of any age) needs to place Kingdom relationships above their family links. That is for them to decide at the right time. We will minister in ways that support and enhance family links, and by our long term contacts perhaps earn the right to be around, and useful, if and when hard decisions about loyalties come up.

So, once again, what seems at first glance to be a straightforward principle (family-related children's ministry) becomes challenging, when ministry with children is committed to excellence.

7. We will encourage and help each child in regular Bible-reading.

As I prepared to write this section, I did some thinking about my own Bible reading. It seems obvious that the attitude, and practice, of significant adults will be crucial to any plan to encourage children in Bible reading. So, how am I tracking in this matter of Bible reading? I read something from Scripture almost every day. I usually accompany that reading with a commentary on the book being read at that moment. Currently I am reading slowly through the book of Revelation, accompanied by the *NIV Application Commentary* on the text.

This approach to Bible reading, for me, is driven by several factors. One is that I have had the privilege of completing several degrees which involved detailed study of parts of the Bible, alongside constant investigation of the Bible's 'big picture' so I need something that stretches me. For me, the greatest impact is made through the mind to the heart. That is, when I get something straight in my mind, I am open to being gripped and moved by truth. I know others go the opposite way, that is, from emotion to truth.

Another factor in my Bible reading is that I am constantly preparing sermons and talks. Whilst I try not to read only for sermons, the fact is that I need to keep an eye on that fact. When I have been challenged by something in the text of Scripture, I am on the way to insights that might be useful to others.

The Bible, for me, is essential to my Christian faith and journey. It is where I find out about God and his ways. It is my source of knowledge about Jesus and his Spirit. I don't worship the Bible, but I do worship the God revealed through the Bible. I want children to become excited about the possibility of finding out about themselves and about God through this amazing book.

So, one way, perhaps the main way, we will encourage regular Bible reading in children is to model with them that this book matters to us. I often will open the Bible in RE classes. This is partly because I want the children to see that there is a source behind what I am telling them. It is also because I want to 'demystify' the Bible in their minds. After all, the Bible is like no other book they encounter, except maybe a dictionary! It looks different, and it seems overwhelming. The attempts to break the Bible down into acceptable 'chunks', with 'Toddler's Bibles' and the like, will, in my opinion, do more harm than good in the long run.

There are helps to assist children in regular Bible reading: Scripture Union publishes many of them. As adults involved in ministry with children, we should be fully aware of the range available. But the key to encouraging regular Bible reading in children is your own attitude and practice!

Two sources that will help us think this through, and apply what we find out are:

Terry Clutterham, *The Adventure Begins* (Scripture Union, 1996)

Rosemary Cox, *Using the Bible with Children* (Grove, 2000)

8. We will seek to follow Jesus in our understanding of children and the Kingdom of God.

Central to this book has been an understanding of the status of the young child before God. The position argued has been mainly, but not solely, based on what Jesus said about children and God's kingdom. He said that God's kingdom belonged to them (Mark 10:14 and Matthew 19:14). In Luke 18:15-17 we noted that babies were included in those of whom it was said 'the kingdom belongs to such as these'.

What does this mean in practice? It has a shaping effect in the head of the person involved in ministry with children. When I was first starting out in such ministry, I attended training conferences. At these I heard from people for whom children were important. I had already seen such people in action: they loved children, and children enjoyed the company of such adults, I observed. But when it came to an outline of the theology of the work being done with children, the big issue was SIN. It was everywhere, and it was the undisputed starting point. Everyone sins, so everyone is a sinner, rightly under the just condemnation of holy God: that was assumed, and even stated from time to time. Children were little adults, as far as this approach was concerned. Even my brain, not well trained in things theological yet, could see that what these people did with children contradicted their theology. They did not, in fact, approach children as Godless, hell-bent individuals. Their attitude towards children was one of acceptance, love and grace. This was what the children picked up, and responded to.

So what was going on? I became convinced that either key players in ministry with children were 'soft' when it came to practice, or they had a hunch about children and God which was different to the 'party line'. You will realise that I came to believe it was the latter. As I did the work that tried to understand what the Bible actually said about children and God, what emerged was a theological base for a practice that had already been happening.

Jesus accepted children as little people to whom God's kingdom belonged from the outset. So should we. We do not ignore sin, nor did Jesus. Matthew 11: 16-19 shows us that Jesus was not naive about children. Here he uses their attitudes to illustrate the gullibility of an adult society.

We will mirror Jesus in our attitude towards children in any ministry with them that pursues excellence. Children readily came to Jesus. Children have always had a special kind of 'radar' that can detect adults who pretend. Jesus actually did love children, and they knew it. Children can still detect any inconsistencies between what is being said and the attitudes behind what is being done.

What is your attitude towards the children it is your privilege to be involved with? Some Christians involved in evangelism give the impression that they don't actually like people. They seem to see other people as targets, not fragile human beings. They can get angry at the slowness to believe that frustrates their outreach.

Are children targets, for you? Or are they people, little people, who need the knowledge and the experiences that will enable them to make informed and ongoing decisions about Jesus? Are you involved in ministry to children, at children, or with children? Which preposition you choose is significant, and shapes much of your ministry.

So you see, when we say that we will seek to follow Jesus in our understanding of children and the Kingdom, we are not just making a theological statement. One of the driving passions of this book is that theology is practical. What we believe shapes our behaviour. That is no less true in ministry with children.

9. We will be realistic about human rebellion against God.

That humanity has rebelled against God is a given for a Christian understanding of things. That children are somehow caught up in that rebellion, and its outcomes, is also a given. What this book has tried to do, amongst other things, is to hold in creative tension the realities of that rebellion and the grace of God, then to apply this to children and their status with God. The position argued is in another chapter: here we want to think about the 'so what' a little more.

I am currently in an interesting debate in my own ministry setting about the Harry Potter phenomenon. The four books (with three more and a movie to come) by J K Rowland have taken publishing, not just children's publishing, by storm. That this is imaginative, funny writing is beyond doubt. Harry Potter is a good read; once started it is hard to put down. That is the experience of adults as well as children. It is not often you see adults openly reading a children's book on public transport!

The issue of controversy is that Harry is a trainee wizard, and the story is based around his years at Hogwarts, an imaginary school for wizards in England. There are schools elsewhere, against whom interesting interschool events are held.

In the minds of some, wizard equals witchcraft, which equals the satan, which equals wrong and against God. Dozens of kids in my RE classes have read Harry Potter books this year, and it is clear that my classes are just like many others. One of my clear strategic understandings of outreach and evangelism is that we need to find a way in, a connection, into the lives of those with whom we want to share Jesus.

So I planned 'A Muggle's Guide To Christmas'. 'Muggles', in Harry Potter books, are ordinary human beings, that is, people without magic powers. So, the program was code for 'An Ordinary Human Being's Guide To Christmas'. The program was about Jesus, and we did not even open a Harry Potter book. But the use of Potter terminology led some church people to ask that the program be dropped, on the grounds that we were endorsing witchcraft, and opening the way into this dimension for children.

There is a Harry Potter website battle going on, based on the evil of the books. You would have to have been on Mars not to be a bit aware of some of the debate. So what has this to do with a section on the reality of sin?

I am no evangelist for Harry Potter, but I am convinced that God has gifted human beings with imagination. The children I have talked with privately in RE know Harry Potter is make believe: they just love the stories, the humour, the action and the undercurrent of irreverence towards adults. The only children who have said anything negative to me have been from

Christian homes. One 8-year-old told me that 'J K Rowland is a satanist'. (It isn't true, by the way.) I feel so sorry for the death of imagination this represents, but even more for the stance of fear it shows. Those spending energy and time opposing the Potter phenomenon seem to be characterised mainly by fear.

If Christian parents want to exercise restraint on their children, that is fine. I support and have guided many parents in thinking through where the boundaries might be, in literature, film, television and computer. That is a whole area for discussion in itself. But when it comes to outreach, bringing the message about Jesus to the majority of children outside the churches, another set of factors come into play.

In that situation, we need imagination and courage. Just as Paul connected to his audience on Mars Hill (Acts 17), by starting in their worldview, we will seek the connecting entry points into the lives of children and their families. Currently, Harry Potter is the 'talk of the town'. Certainly the subject matter has an 'edge' to it, but the gospel can stand up in any market place, including the Harry Potter market place. There is no way Paul endorsed the philosophies of the Greeks at Mars Hill. He simply used them to connect with people, so he could get them to Jesus. The challenge of Harry Potter will not go away. There are at least two movies and three more books to come. The most balanced discussion published so far is: *What's A Christian To Do With Harry Potter*, by Connie Neal, Waterbrook Press, 2001.

10. We will work hard to strengthen nurture, especially in the home and in the church.

Potentially, the main nurturers of spirituality in children are their parents. To do this, the parents must have their own spirituality, of course. The local church, the 'family of families', can supplement the home. Or it can supply what the home does not have, if the child is from a setting in which spiritual matters are absent, or treated with indifference.

So there are two main sources of nurture. When both are working well, Christian nurture is a wonderful adventure. If both are failing, Christian nurture is absent. If the two are pulling against each other, the result is confusion. Let it be said, in a hushed whisper, that not all Christian parents involve themselves in much planned spiritual nurture of their children. Some get themselves so caught up in careers, study and/or church activities that the survival of their marriages, not the quality of their children's spiritual life, becomes a priority. Or does not become a priority. I have watched, helplessly, too many marriages drift apart, as the couple lives what becomes a parallel life. They apparently believe that God will somehow 'work things out'.

We do not accidentally fulfill our obligations as parents. Not only are we accountable to God for our parenting, our children will often 'playback', as on video, the attitudes and actions we have demonstrated. There is not, of course, a direct relationship between our input and their output. There are any number of other influences on our kids, not least the unique mix that makes up their own personalities. The mystery is that we can live consistent Christian lives with our kids and they still might reject all that matters most to us. We need to care for each other, in the church, when this is happening. To do that, we need to learn how to be open with each other. Parents whose children are 'moving on with the Lord' need to forego any sense of smugness, or assuming that there will never be a 'crunch-time' in their kid's lives.

Programs that don't pretend about parenting will nurture truly. We don't need to wallow in painful hypothetical possibilities. There are enough real situations to deal with in any congregation where honesty about parenting has become normal behaviour.

11. We will nurture our own walk with Christ.

Just before settling down to write this section, I was reading 'Hope for Children in Crisis', in the journal of *Rainbows of Hope*, a Christian organisation committed to ministry, and support of ministry, with children 'at the edge'. In an article on work among street kids in Brazil, the author writes movingly, and honestly, about some of the struggles in helping street kids through the stages that will mean they can successfully leave behind street life.

There is a comment about the uniqueness of each child. Then the boundaries within which a child must be willing to operate, if they are to stay in the program are set out. Then comes this comment:

'When a child is rebellious and will not contribute to the day-to-day life or is disruptive, workers will spend time encouraging him or her to value this opportunity. If the child is not making progress after weeks or months or perhaps starts to regress, we consider his or her case and sometimes the outcome is to move him or her on. Often, spiritual warfare and fasting on the children's behalf transforms their situations.'

A little later in the article, the fact that work with families is one of the most important aspects of the ministry is noted. Home visits are central to this:

'Home visits are an important part of the children's lives, not only to prepare them and their families for the time when they will live together again, but also to keep the children from becoming too attached to their life in an institution. Sometimes these weekend visits can be very upsetting and much time is spent in counselling and praying for the children and their families.'

Here is a ministry that nurtures its own spirituality. Then, from that base it naturally turns to the spiritual dimension in the rough and tumble of face-to-face ministry.

If we are to be used by God in ministry with children, the quality of our own walk with Christ will be a major factor in the quality of that ministry. One would have thought this was obvious. God can, and does, do things beyond the contribution of his servants. God is not bound by us. But the sensitivity that comes from a close walk with Christ, the discernment that flows from being in tune with the Spirit, and the love that comes out of a heart full of the love of God, enhances and enables excellence to become part of our ministry. And we are 'on' about excellence, are we not?

12. We will depend, finally, on the Holy Spirit, not techniques.

In our ministry with children and their families, we will develop and strengthen whatever skills will contribute to the quality of that ministry. Some of the skills will be techniques, insights that will enable us to better handle groups of children, or better communicate with both children and adults. For example, some of the conflict resolution strategies I have been trained in have become important for dealing with parents. Active listening is a skill, with some techniques (like 'I' statements), applying to communication in general, not just when conflict is evident. Learning that making statements instead of asking questions is an excellent technique in front of any large group of children, has saved me several times. It has also helped a number of other people over the years. But, when all is said and done, techniques like these are means, not ends. The reason I want to have the attention of a crowd of children is what matters, not the control, in and of itself. Some people can get control of groups of children to enthuse them about a new toy, or a food. Techniques are neutral at best: any work that is going to last must be done by the Holy Spirit.

So what is our role? 2 Corinthians 4:1-7 is a key passage about ministry. We are to 'set forth the truth plainly', refusing to use deception, or 'shameful ways', including the manipulation of emotions. The image Paul develops in this passage is of a cosmic battle between 'the god of this age' (the satan) and the God who said 'Let light shine out of darkness'. The god of this age blinds people: the God and Father of our Lord Jesus Christ shines into the minds and lives of people. Maybe we should just let them fight it out? No, says Paul. Into the midst of this cosmic battle, and in some way part of the work of God, 'we preach'. What we preach (I take it that 'preach', here, means any communication of the gospel, not just pulpit preaching) is 'Jesus Christ as Lord'. Our lives demonstrate this by the fact that we become servants (slaves) of those to whom we preach That is, the lordship of Christ is both what controls our lifestyle and is our message.

This is well beyond technique! We will make use of any insights that will help us connect better into the lives of those with whom we wish to share the gospel, including children and their families. And we will subordinate all skills and techniques to the work of the Holy Spirit. Which means that sometimes we will not use some techniques, because they do not sit easily with the Spirit.

For example, I once saw an adult working with a group of children at the end of a week-long camp. We were at a last night campfire. Something had happened which had raised the emotional climate in the group. The adult worked emotions up even more, then told a story about someone who put off 'responding to Christ' (sic), and who was killed on the way home from a meeting. On the basis of this, he appealed to the children to 'give their hearts to Jesus' right away. I was appalled, but I was a junior leader. Talking afterwards with kids who responded only confirmed to me that they had been scared into something. They were not sure what the 'something' was!

I think anyone in tune with Spirit would have toned down the emotions at this camp-fire, not stirred them up. I also believe the responses God would have drawn from a 'toned-down' situation would have lasted longer than some of those given that night. This is not a criticism of the kids, nor is it saying that we never should stress urgency. But if the work that lasts is from God, not us, we need to 'back off' sometimes, and leave the field to him.

13. We will improve our story-telling ability.

It might seem, at first glance, that this section contradicts the last one. Is not storytelling a technique? Whilst there are techniques that will enhance the art of storytelling, the practice of storytelling is, in itself, much more than a bundle of techniques.

In storytelling we encounter one of the most powerful mediums of human communication. The message of the Bible is told as a story: it is God's 'big story'. The relationship of our own 'little story' to God's 'big story' is one way to think about the gospel. The idea that our little story can be linked to, be drawn into, God's big story is amazing good news.

I think there is a difference between 'telling a story' and 'being a storyteller'. Both are important. Telling stories, in the sense of making something come alive to children, is a crucial skill for those who minister with children and their families. Stories are 'about' something. It could be the story of the birth of Jesus, the crossing of the Red Sea, the shipwreck of Paul or the tower of Babel. Something that happened, either historically or imaginatively (Narnia stories, for example) is presented as a story.

When we do this, we will often introduce 'angles' into the story, angles that go beyond a text, yet remain true to the text. For example, I have a story about a gravedigger who waited for a funeral that never arrived. This allows me to tell the story of the raising of the widow's son by Jesus at Nain (Luke 7) in a way that seems to engage the imaginations of children. There are many 'angle' approaches to the Christmas story, as adults seek ways into the imagination of children for a story that has become too familiar for many of them.

In the art of telling stories, one technique is to prepare a grid of potential 'angles' from which to approach the story, and then choose the most suitable. So, in the Christmas story, we could tell it from the angle of Mary, Joseph, the inn-keeper, the inn-keeper's daughter, a shepherd who went to the stable, a shepherd who stayed behind to mind the sheep, the manger, a donkey, Herod, someone staying at the inn who was woken up...and so it goes on.

When we use this approach in telling stories, we have to exercise discipline. We are committed to being true to the story. We can't just let our imagination 'run riot'. We have to do our homework. We want to engage the minds and the imaginations of our audience, and introduce them to something that happened, and to do it all in a memorable way. In fact 'memorable' is perhaps the word for telling stories. Lodging something in the minds of other people in ways that will stay in their memories.

If this is anything near the centre of an understanding of what it means to tell stories, what is the difference in 'being a storyteller'? Storytellers remain themselves and speak directly to their audience. The subject matter is their own life, or an experience in the life of someone else, an experience that becomes the basis of an interpersonal encounter between the storyteller and the audience. When such an encounter has depth and substance, the relationship established takes on a sacred character.

I have had some good moments when telling stories, 'aha' moments when children have connected to something very strongly. I remember last year, as I finished a retelling of the parable of the prodigal son/waiting father/elder brother from Luke 15. I finished where Jesus did, with the older brother still outside the party. One boy said, 'Did he go to the party?' I said, 'I don't know. That's where Jesus ended the story.' Before I could ask him what he thought, the boy offered the comment, 'Well, it's a really good story!' I think we had connected!

On the other hand, there is another dimension when we are a storyteller, not just telling stories, however well we might do that. During a lesson last year, it became relevant to tell the children about a cancer operation I faced a few years ago. I told them it was a life-threatening operation. I told them that I had written a letter to my sons in case I did not survive. I also said that I was scared at one point, then really calm, as I realised God was with me. The connection was strong, and it was at another level.

If we are going to tell good Bible stories, we need to immerse ourselves in the Bible. We need to go to training opportunities, and to practice new techniques. If we are going to tell stories, let us do it excellently.

If we are going to be a storyteller, there is a further challenge. Storytellers, those who are committed to speaking directly, with the aim of personal encounter, will need to be at ease with themselves. Disclosing oneself in any way, particularly vulnerably, comes out of security. Jesus is the great storyteller and John 13:4 is the insight into his security. Jesus knew who he was, and out of that security he was able to be a vulnerable servant.

'Jesus knew that the Father had put all things under his power, and that he had come from God and was returning to God; so he got up from the meal, took off his outer clothing, and wrapped a towel around his waist.' (John 13:4)

14. We will study the world of children and the world of the Bible.

One clear outcome of what has been said so far in this section is that if we are committed to excellence in ministry with children, we will study both the world of children and the world of the Bible. This is because our aim, under God, is to bring these two worlds together. What 'study' means will differ for each of us, of course. Some will want to do courses; some will want to participate in training opportunities; some will read material they know will help. Whatever it means, it is the attitude underneath that matters. As far as we can, to the best of our ability, we want to know these two worlds.

So, if I am involved with eight year olds, I will include knowing about the fads, the books, the films, and the TV programs that matter to that age right now. Not so I can become an 'expert' in these things. Simply so I can connect with the children. It was fascinating to witness the excitement in the RE classes last year, as a number of children and I read the Harry Potter books at the same time. We talked about different scenes before the actual RE lessons started. They liked the idea that this adult enjoyed what they were enjoying.

At the same time, I keep working on materials that will help me understand the Bible better, and open up fresh ways of teaching from it. One interesting dimension to this challenge is in the use of language. If we are really 'receiver-friendly' we will keep working at the jargon we use, changing it to plain English. One simple example came last week, in a story about prayer based on the healing of the daughter who died while Jesus was coming to her. I told the children that in those days you could pay people 'to cry for you' when someone had died. I said this instead of talking about 'mourners', a word I know the children would not understand. A little example, but typical of an attitude and an approach.

Over the years I have often said that if we are to explain the meaning of the death of Jesus to a child, we need to understand the theology of the death of Christ at depth. Teaching children about God is not the 'soft option'. We need to be the best we can, then make ourselves available for him to use us.

15. We will seek to develop critical openness in each child.

This interesting phrase 'critical openness' was used in a British report about children in the church, published in the 1980s. It holds together, in a creative tension, two important dimensions in ministry with children that is committed to excellence.

On the one hand, we want to teach children and lead them in other ways that will leave them with an attitude of expectancy about God. 'Openness' is a good way to describe this. On the other hand, we want children to be questioners, and to know that God, and we, welcome their questions. 'Critical' is a good word for this, in the sense that the children will be encouraged to question things. They will anyway, so it is better if we let them know it is ok to do so!

Some adults still seem to think that children are better off protected from questions. 'Simply tell them the truth', they say. The result of this attitude and approach will, of course, make children dependent. If there are no adults present to give the answers, they end up confused, or just naive. Education today is based on questioning and research. We must not expect children, or people of any age, to park their brain when matters to do with God are on the agenda. I can remember my earliest experience of this attitude. I came into a Christian youth fellowship from outside the church. I watched as a couple of young university students raised questions each Friday night, and saw them 'squashed' each time. 'Christians believe, not question', they were told. I wonder where those people are, in relation to God, today?

It is fascinating to watch children come alive as they realise we are not only open to their questions, but we have some good ones ourselves! That is, the critical openness' that we want to grow in children will be demonstrated by us. It will be caught, as much as it is taught. It is certainly the approach that has the best possibility of lasting the distance in the lives of the children. Brainwashing lasts as long as the next stronger personality: critical openness can even push back against brainwashing.

16. We will discipline, in the context of love.

I remember one wonderful Bible class I taught a few years ago. The group, when we formed it, was made up of kids in early secondary schooling. They were thirsty for the things of God. We stayed together for two years, and they opened up like flowers. I suppose the teaching was ok, but it was God who was at work! There was never a discipline issue in the group. They were motivated and involved. As they moved on to another teacher, I was to take over a new group of kids in early secondary schooling. The first week set the scene. It was as if they had decided that I would not do to them what had been done to the other group. They weren't really sure what had been done to the others, but they knew they did not want it!

There were discipline issues from the outset. Lateness, rudeness, sullenness, and absences: it all came. I lasted about six weeks, and then surrendered. However much I rationalised it from my lifestyle at the time, I let them down. I think the earlier experience had stayed with me, and I could not be patient to build again.

'There is no such thing as an inattentive child' is a line that always gets a reaction at training events. People can be quite vehement in their rejection of the idea. That is until we think it through a bit, and then they will usually readily agree that a child is always being attentive to something. By definition, when they are not attending to what I want them focused on, I have a 'discipline' issue!

So, the key to preventing discipline problems is to run interesting programs. That will not 'solve' all problems of discipline, of course. Illness, worry, pain, low self-esteem and anger, are all sources for discipline problems. When we are involved in ministry with real children, we will face the matter of discipline at some point.

How we respond to discipline challenges is crucial to our ministry. We will model something significant as we respond to pressure. The behaviours and attitudes we think create discipline problems are points of pressure for us in ministry. They are moments when we are not in control, when our plans are not working, or when someone is pushing against our authority. Children learn a great deal from watching adults under pressure. And they do watch! Some of the things they see and hear are very sad. Sometimes they see Christian adults with very short fuses, who raise their voices and quickly get upset. Children in the primary school ages have a highly developed sense of fairness. They will be upset if they believe the adult is being unfair in their response to a discipline matter. They may even be disturbed that something is thought to be a discipline issue.

In a ministry characterised by excellence, there will be discipline. The discipline will be motivated by love, the 'God' kind of love that demands the best from people. We will not threaten to do anything that we are not willing to carry out. So we will not speak about consequences except when we are at peace with God about the matter. We will respond, rather than just react, to situations.

It is all too possible to think that love has no boundaries. Often the kids themselves want boundaries, even around love. I remember leading a Sunday School team many years ago, which we operated on Sunday afternoons at a girls' home in the suburbs of Sydney. The girls all came from some kind of broken home. We brought unjudging love to them; the only time most of them had ever experienced it. They nearly 'gobbled us up'. They wanted to touch us all the time. Leaving was a very emotional moment every Sunday afternoon. Some of the team was sure we must not discipline the girls, knowing about some of the experiences they had been through. But we came to realise that we had to establish some boundaries. This was not just for our own sakes, but because real love, including God's love, has boundaries. It was not easy, because many of the girls associated any kind of restrictions with lack of love. A number of the team found out that they had a similar attitude. None of us were parents, which probably speaks volumes for our attitudes at the time!

It became a great learning experience for all of us. We learned to discipline in the context of love. The girls learned that discipline can be associated with unconditional love. It was able to happen because the girls knew we cared about them. The team gained a new understanding about accountability in a Christian setting. We didn't even know the word 'accountability' in those days! Looking back, I now know that we practised it, as we stumbled towards an understanding of the practice of discipline with love. We learned that it means: not shouting at people; listening carefully to people; checking what they think we said, or did; checking what we think they said, or did; responding not just reacting. But it also meant that there were some definite boundaries, beyond which was the 'no go' area of behaviour.

The outcome? Security. The girls felt secure, many of them in ways that they had never experienced before with adults. It was not that we did not ever have any discipline challenges again, but they were responded to in the context of tough love. The girls knew we loved them, because we treated them as important enough to discipline with that kind of love.

17. We will include fun and feelings in our ministry with children.

Some Christians in ministry are so serious they are like chloroform to enjoyment. Now, 'enjoyment' is not the only goal of Christian ministry, let's grant that right away. But neither is boring people out of their socks the goal.

Any ministry with children that has no fun dimension is heading for trouble, if not disaster. Very often, fun is the crossover point of connection into the lives of children. I have a ventriloquist doll called Archie. I am not very good at it, even after 30 years, but I remain amazed at the power of the connection Archie allows me to make with groups of children. We don't have to have a doll like Archie, of course. Children have a fascinating 'radar' that picks up whether or not the adult in front of them is a 'fun' person or not. They can detect hypocrisy from about two kilometres. They go into reverse in the company of people who are 'too serious'.

Then there are feelings. In some Christian circles, we are so focused on thinking, and correctness, that we forget about imagination and feelings. Whilst it is possible to analyse love, it is, first and foremost, something to be experienced. Many people 'feel' their way into the kingdom of God, moved inside by acts of love, or a deep longing that is beyond words. They may learn to put words to their experiences later, and that is a good thing, but the journey often begins in feelings, not in words.

Excellent ministry with children will always treat children as whole human beings. Not just as minds, and not just as bundles of emotions, but as 'feelings that can think' and 'thinking that can feel'. It is that combination which takes us into the dimension of imagination, one of the essential ingredients of the kingdom of God.

Following the example of Jesus, Christian ministry with children that is excellent will have flair, imagination and fun in it. It will stimulate, not stultify, the minds and the imaginations of the children. In doing so, it will first have stimulated the minds and imaginations of the adults involved in ministry. Yet another reason for doing children's ministry!

18. We will model the gospel, as well as teach it.

This principle of excellent ministry with children is a statement of fact. We will model a gospel. All Christians model a version of the gospel through the words and attitudes they display in their lives.

So, what version of the gospel do you want your children to see? The story is told of the Sunday School teacher who was having a bad morning. Johnny, especially, was a pain. He was fidgety, whispering and inattentive. The teacher took it for a while, getting hotter and hotter. Finally, he shouted, 'Johnny, shut up! Can't you see that I'm trying to teach you about the love of God!' A gospel had been modelled! Guess what the class remembered that week.

Earlier we referred to 2 Corinthians 4:5, the verse that connects the message and the lifestyle of evangelism.

'For we do not preach ourselves, but Jesus Christ as Lord, with ourselves as your servants for Jesus' sake.'

Servanthood is the key to the gospel. God Almighty entered our world as a servant. This is powerfully set out in Philippians 2:5-8.

'[Christ Jesus] who, being in very nature God, did not consider equality with God something to be grasped, but made himself nothing, taking the form of a servant, being made in human likeness. And being found in appearance as a man, he humbled himself and became obedient to death - even death on a cross!'

We are servants of the children in our care. If that idea has gripped us, and controls our actions, we will model the true gospel. When Christian attitudes and actions coincide, powerful and excellent ministry takes place.

19. We will be alert to special problems, and know how to refer.

Because we Christians have been made wide awake by the Holy Spirit, we know we live in a world that is beautiful and ugly at the same time. We know that there are things done in this world that shame all of us. Sometimes, sadly, we will face this in ministry with children.

In any work amongst children in our society today, it is 'possible that we will face the question of abuse, or at least the suspicion of abuse. Or we may find ourselves dealing with a child who is stressed, or even depressed. Or we may find ourselves trying to include a hyperactive child in group activities. All of these situations are examples of boundaries of expertise in ministry with children. In an excellent ministry we will know where the boundaries are. We will also know where to go for information about networks that include the kind of special training and experience that can respond to children with particular needs.

Most ministers will have a referral list, and are open to the inclusion of more people who have expertise with children. Our request that this be part of the church's referral network may be the trigger for it to happen. People with expertise with adults do not necessarily relate well to children. There are skills and knowledge special to children's needs. We will refer prayerfully and carefully, of course. We will do it in consultation with our ministers, so that we are accountable for what we are doing and so that the bigger picture is always in view.

That we include this dimension in a discussion of excellence in ministry with children is evidence of an understanding of gospel ministry that includes all aspects of a child's life. An important, and lovely, biblical word from the Old Testament is 'shalom'. This is a word that describes wholeness, peace, being integrated, having God at the centre. Any gospelling that has 'shalom' in it has the goal of people operating as whole persons. That is God's original design and plan. The gospel is about reconciliation and restoration. God is in the rewiring and rebuilding business. God takes minds that need rewiring and lives that need rebuilding, then makes something beautiful out of those our lives. Those lives might, probably do, include emotional and other kinds of scars, but God has a way of weaving even scars together in a way that brings out beauty.

The attitude that drives ministry with children informed by this kind of outlook was captured by a speaker at a Scripture Union international conference some years ago.

'While there remains a single child in the world who is denied their rights in God, we will not cease from our strivings to help them or to encourage others to do so. While there are children imprisoned in the blackness of urban deprivation, or who face the horrors of wars, famine or drought, while there are children whose spirits are trapped in false religions or ideologies, our work must go on.'

20. We will pursue excellence in our ministry with children.

The leaders of our world in the year 2030 are alive and about 10 years old right now. Children matter in their own right, but add this dimension and the strategic value of children's ministry becomes breathtaking.

It is also a fact of our own life that we only have one of them (life that is!), so we will not want to waste gifting, training and ministry. Once we have settled the idea that we have some kind of calling to ministry with children, how can we be committed to anything less than excellence?

Let it be noted that there is a difference between excellence and perfection. We are committed to the pursuit of excellence, not perfection. There will be moments, maybe many, of satisfaction in our ministry, when children respond with excitement about Jesus. When the gleam in the eyes is without guile or guilt, just acceptance and openness. When a little hand of trust enters yours.

But there are likely to be moments of despair and disappointment. When they come, the test of the direction of our ministry comes to us. If we are committed to perfection, we will fail regularly. If we pursue excellence, we can absorb failure, allow God to train us in and through it, then continue the pursuit.

Go out and pursue excellence. God deserves nothing less. Nor do the children.

Resources

that will assist the pursuit of excellence in ministry with children and their families.

The following materials are listed according to the author's name, alphabetically. Some are more central than others, of course. So # is used to indicate the publications that, in my opinion, are ones to seek after first. There are many more resources available, but this is not simply a bibliography, listing as many publications as possible. If you would like information about publications that explore specific issues in more depth, or you would like to think about some of the theological or developmental matters more, contact me through the publisher.

The criteria for inclusion in this list are that the publication deals with a central issue in an interesting way, and/or provides practical ideas for ministry. As far as I know, all the materials are still in print.

Barfield, Maggie, *Let's Sing and Shout!* , Scripture Union, 1998. (250 songs, rhymes and prayers to use with young children.)

Bell, David, *Mission Possible*, Scripture Union/CPAS, 2000. (Lots of ideas and resources for evangelism with children.)

Bridger, Francis, *Children Finding Faith*, Scripture Union/CPAS, 2000 edition. (A strong case for bringing together the insights from developmental studies and theology in our ministries with children.)

Chapman, Gary and Campbell, Ross, *The Five Love Languages of Children*, Moody Press, 1997. (A great tool that helps us relate to individual children in ways that acknowledges their uniqueness.)

Chapman, Gary, *The Five Love Languages of Teenagers*, Northfield Publishing, 2000. (The same tool applied to teens.)

Cloud, Henry and Townsend, John, *Boundaries With Kids*, Strand Publishing, 1998. (Strategies for developing responsibility in children.)

Cloud, Henry and Townsend, John, *Boundaries With Kids Workbook*, Zondervan Publishing, 1998. (The application of the strategies.)

Copsey, Kathryn, *Here's One I Made Earlier*, Scripture Union, 1995. (Craft resources for 3s to 11s.)

Dawn, Marva, *Is It A Lost Cause?*, Eerdmans, 1997. (An in-depth, passionate, plea for the inclusion of children in the community of faith.)

Donaldson, Margaret, *Children's Minds*, Fontana, 1978. (The work which challenges many of the assumptions about what children can and can't do in their thinking.)

Frank, Penny, *Bringing Children To Faith*, Scripture Union /CPAS, 2000. (A handbook about training adults in evangelism with children.)

Hay, David, *The Spirit of the Child*, HarperCollins, 1998. (A detailed look at the spirituality of children outside the church, in England.)

Kilbourn, Phyllis (ed), *Children In Crisis*, MARC, 1996. (An introduction to ministries with children 'on the edge'.)

Komp, Diane, *Images of Grace*, Zondervan, 1996 (What Komp has learned from children dying of cancer.)

Lane, John (ed), *Gospelling to the Beat 1*, Scripture Union, 1998. (50 songs for use with children in mission situations.)

Lane, John (ed), *Gospelling to the Beat 2*, Scripture Union, 1999. (50 more songs for mission situations.)

LeFever, Marlene, *Learning Styles*, Kingsway Publications, 1995. (A detailed introduction to the different ways people learn, and the implications for those who would teach.)

Merrell, Judith, *How To Cheat At Visual Aids!*, Scripture Union, 1996. (Visual aids, using the artwork of Pauline Adams, all available to copy.)

Stonehouse, Catherine, *Joining Children on the Spiritual Journey*, Baker Books, 1998. (Places the emphasis where it should be, for those who would want to minister with children.)